OVIDIU DRAGOŞ ARGEŞANU

ABOUT ANGELS

Questions and Answers

OVIDIU DRAGOȘ ARGEȘANU

ABOUT ANGELS

Questions and Answers

PRO DAO

About Angels—Questions and Answers

Pro Dao Publishing House
ISBN 978-606-9721-19-3

www.edituraprodao.ro
www.ovidiudragosargesanu.ro

Copy editing:
Book design by: Arthur Weber
Cover design by: Mihai Moldoveanu
Front cover image by: Freepik.com

Publishing Services by www.edituravirtuala.ro

"*There are angels*—they are everywhere around you! You are deeply loved, supported, and guided by many Heavenly beings, and you have nothing to fear."

"Angel Numbers 101"—Doreen Virtue

My thanks go to Carmen,
without whom this book would not exist.

ABOUT ANGELS

In the vast expanse of our Universe, humanity does not stand alone. We share this cosmic realm with spiritual entities, ethereal and intangible, commonly referred to as angels.

This tome draws its inspiration from ***MyAngels***, a platform conceived by visionary souls yearning for a profound connection with the cosmos and a collective journey through life, guided and supported by celestial beings. It is a manifestation of desires kindled within a community of seekers, along with their inquiries about angels. These inquiries have been meticulously transcribed into the form of questions and answers, ensuring accessibility and utility to readers of diverse ages and levels of enlightenment. My aspiration for this volume is to serve as a pragmatic guide to the enigmatic realm of angels.

Our exploration of angels traverses a comprehensive spectrum, commencing from their very inception, navigating through the fall of select celestial entities, their myriad typologies, distinct characteristics, and nuanced attributes. We delve into the subtle signs of their celestial presence, probe their celestial mission, contemplate their ethereal visage, explore their intrinsic nature, and unravel their divine purpose. Our journey even extends to the complex framework of their celestial hierarchy.

However, it is imperative to clarify that I shall not tread upon the well-trodden path of angelology, the scholarly discipline dedicated to the biblical portrayal of angels, as elucidated in Hebrews 1:14: "Are they not all ministering spirits, sent forth to minister for them who shall be heirs of salvation?"

In our modern era, diverse perspectives, some diverging from the biblical narrative, have emerged concerning angels. Some posit that angels are the spirits of departed mortals, serving as our spiritual guides. Others perceive angels as impersonal sources of metaphysical power that we may harness, while a few steadfastly deny the very existence of angels. Yet others assert their exclusive privilege to access angels and the ethereal dimensions from which they emanate.

The noble purpose of this compendium is to address the elemental queries that have arisen regarding the celestial realm of angels, elucidating their interaction with humankind and their unwavering dedication to the divine designs of the Creator.

1. What is the association between angels and the MyAngels platform?

The genesis of the MyAngels platform can be traced back to the earnest aspiration of uniting benevolent, optimistic individuals, wholeheartedly committed to the cause of good. Their objective: to amplify the influence of their angels in assisting people to actualise their dreams, attain wisdom, progress on a spiritual plane, and nurture their material, mental, and spiritual prosperity. The overarching aim is to bind virtuous souls together in mutual emotional sustenance, orchestrated through the agency of their souls, their angels, and the Divine Creator.

2. Why was a compendium of questions and answers pertaining to angels deemed necessary?

For an extended period, the existence of angels was shrouded in obscurity, for acknowledging their presence inherently entailed human self-discovery. It necessitated an understanding of one's essence, identity amidst the realms of Earth and Heaven, and proficiency in communicating and collaborating with angels, all in the pursuit of spiritual ascension and the fulfilment of dreams, thus enhancing life's splendour through angelic intervention.

3. What constitutes the essence of angels?

Angels embody immortal entities, spiritual beings characterised by either luminous or shadowed countenance.

4. When and by whom were angels ushered into existence?

Angels, entities of enduring nature, were conceived by the hand of God before the dawn of all existence and the inception of time itself. Their existence is perennial. These celestial beings were conjured into being during the inaugural of the six days, when God proclaimed, "Let there be light." Within this luminance, angels found their inception, prior to all other ephemeral beings - humankind, fauna, insects, avians, and the entirety of the encompassing natural world.

5. What pertains to the nexus between angels and the particle of God?

The particle of God symbolises the primordial seed from which the tapestry of existence is woven. It emanates as a radiant luminescence birthed by the Holy Spirit. Angels, in their entirety, are hewn from the mosaic of divine particles.

6. Do angels, in their celestial sojourn, harbour volition, or do they chart their course solely under the aegis of divine orchestration?

Every spiritual entity, inclusive of demons, is endowed with volition. Yet, one must comprehend that the sole entity vested with unadulterated free will is the Primordial God; all others grapple with circumscribed autonomy. Angels, consequently, exercise free will, their birthright bestowed by God from inception, together with the mantle of decision-making. Nevertheless, the intrinsic nature of angels, coupled with their assigned purpose at creation, imposes certain constraints. Notwithstanding, just as Lucifer, once among the heavenly host, exercised his choice, so may any angel.

7. Do angels, beings of celestial origin, emerge from the forge of perfection?

Perfection eludes angels, a testament to God's bequest of free will, which endows them with the capacity for deviation.

8. Does the mantle of pride drape the angels from their genesis?

Indeed, the vestiges of pride resonate within the celestial sphere. Its germination took root concomitant with the descent of certain angelic brethren. Those who remained unscathed perceived themselves as preeminent.

9. What does the phrase "May God shield you from the pride of angels" signify?

The angels who opted to remain in the service of the Divine developed a hubris that led them to believe that every decision they made was inherently righteous. Consequently, when provoked or contradicted, an angel not only experiences indignation but also tends to nurture a disposition for retaliation. Instances of such interactions can be found in sacred texts, notably in the account of the father of John the Baptist, among others. This principle holds true even in the case of angels who have incarnated.

10. Do angels possess an EGO?

First and foremost, let us establish the nature of the EGO, so as to avoid conflating it with pride. The EGO is comprised of all the narratives that traverse our minds, narratives to which we attach our identities: criticism, controversy, judgment, fantasy, mockery, adoration, trivialisation, and the like. These narratives give rise to the subjective realities unique to each individual. Specifically, guardian angels may become ensnared in this phenomenon if they misconstrue, interpret, or subjectively grasp or experience situations or individuals, which could lead to their descent to Earth for incarnation.

11. What unfolds when an angel, through the exercise of free will, elects not to align with the Divine will?

Such a choice culminates in the angelic descent. Analogous to God's awareness of Lucifer's stratagem and His allowance of free will, the moment of Lucifer's defeat precipitated his expulsion from the celestial realm, subsequently initiating the downfall of Lucifer along with all the angels who had cast their lot with him.

12. Where can one find the angels?

The material world exists at the crossroads of light and shadow, where beings of both light and darkness dwell. Within our material realm, angels are ubiquitous; they coexist among us and reside within us.

13. Why has the Christian Church refrained from delving into the realm of angels?

The answer lies in the profound implications that understanding angels entails. For once a soul comprehends the celestial realm, it gains access to knowledge, healing, power, glimpses of the beyond, the tapestry of time—past and future—all of which extends beyond the scope the Church of Jesus Christ desires for its flock. The Church sought to retain sole dominion over matters of spiritual discourse, encouraging prayer to guardian angels and heavenly powers, such as Michael and Gabriel. Yet, it discouraged direct communion or meditation with angels as intermediaries with God, ensuring that the Christian priest remained the sole conduit for divine interaction.

14. What comprises the essence of angels?

Angels, like all elements within the spiritual and material spheres, are crafted from particles, information, energy, and spirit.

15. How do angels manifest their appearance?

Angels, as spiritual entities, lack corporeal forms. Instead, they adopt specific visages that align with their hierarchical roles and specialties, facilitating the fulfilment of their divine missions. While many angels take on forms akin to humans, devoid of wings and featuring masculine, feminine, or childlike attributes, others are resplendent with wings—two, four, or even six—and may bear either the radiance of light or the shadow of darkness.

16. Do all angels possess wings?

Not all angels bear wings, as angels, by nature, lack physical forms. They assume tangible forms to make themselves perceptible to human senses. While many angels resemble humans without wings, most are adorned with wings, be it two, four, or six, and these wings may accompany angels of both light and darkness.

17. What is the quantity of angels?

The precise number of angels eludes human comprehension. The Apostle John's Revelation attests to this mystery, as he heard the voices of countless angels—myriads upon myriads and thousands upon thousands. The Bible also speaks of "heavenly hosts," numbering tens of thousands and millions of angels, constituting multitudes beyond measure, akin to legions.

18. Is Earth a testing ground for Heaven and angels, and what role do angels play in this scenario?

Earth stands as a convergence point for a myriad of

celestial interests: 1. It serves as the battleground for the eternal struggle between good and evil, where angels and demons vie for dominance. 2. It acts as a crucible for assessing faith and spiritual virtues. 3. Earth becomes the harvest ground for souls. 4. Here, divine skirmishes unfold as different gods vie for ownership of souls. 5. Spiritual treasures are unearthed amid earthly trials. 6. Demons and angels are dispatched here for education. Angels, sometimes, bear the penance of descending to Earth, while others embark on educational sojourns, and still others revel in moments of levity.

19. Can angels attain enlightenment?

Angels, devoid of innate light, derive their luminance from the God to whom they are bound. Enlightenment is an aspiration achievable solely through incarnation. Thus, the desire for earthly embodiment is a universal yearning among all angels.

20. Can angels betray or accuse others?

Angels of light remain bound by the inability to speak untruths or negative realities. Betrayal and accusation are exclusive to the domain of the fallen angel—the celestial entity that has deviated from its divine path and embraced darkness.

21. What constitutes dark angels, and how do they diverge from their luminous counterparts?

Dark angels are, at their essence, creations of God, like their radiant counterparts, serving the divine purpose. For God encompasses both light and darkness within His being. When God declared, "Let there be light," He cleaved light from the shadows, thereby birthing darkness. In response, some angels, the luminous ones, gravitated toward the light, while others, the dark angels, remained within the shadows. Both sets of angels remain in the service of God. Angels of light minister to the luminary aspect of God, while dark angels attend to the shadowed aspect of His being. Angels of darkness are instrumental in delineating boundaries between dimensions. In celestial parlance, there exist "anti-heavens" (distinct from hells; anti-heavens encompass the luminous heavens and the anti-heavens within the dark cosmos), each characterised by the varying quantity of dark particles. Dark angels, in essence, exude benevolence, possessing maximal fundamental beneficial energy (a concept in radiesthesia) but with inner light—often referred to as DH, with a negative connotation. The lower the DH value, the deeper their connection to a broader anti-heaven.

22. What is the mission of dark angels?

The mission of dark angels is to prevent demons from ascending to the higher heavens or descending to Earth. They act as a barrier, obstructing demons from crossing between lower and higher dimensions. Therefore, they stand as the frontline warriors of God in the spiritual realm, closest to the demons.

23. How many varieties of dark angels exist?

There exist three categories of dark angels: the threshold angels, the angels who fell during the era of Enoch and Azazel, and the angels who persist in descending even in the present, for they have erred in some manner. They have descended upon Earth and are compelled to remain here until the Earth's ultimate judgment. All dark angels are angels of black.

24. What are threshold angels?

Threshold angels are the celestial sentinels positioned between Heaven and Earth. They serve as guardians of the celestial boundaries, preventing demons from escaping the lower heavens and guiding departed negative spirits to their appropriate afterlife destinations.

25. What do fallen angels from Azazel's time look like?

Fallen angels from the era of Azazel have only lost their divine radiance, retaining their other angelic attributes. Their appearance still mirrors that of angels.

26. How can fallen angels from Azazel's time return to God?

To return to God, fallen angels must first possess a genuine desire for reconciliation and choose to align with His divine will. We, as humans, can aid in their return through practices like Reiki or neoReiki initiations, or even through Christian baptism. These initiations transcend the material realm, encompassing a spiritual component, and can be extended to any entity, including demons seeking redemption.

27. Do the dark angels refer to those who fell during Lucifer's time?

No, they do not. The fallen angels, commencing with Lucifer's descent, belong to the ranks of the celestial light. After their fall, they transformed into serpents, scorpions, and dragons, among other forms. Dark angels, on the other hand, are distinguished by their distinctive dark hue, ranging from shades of gray to deep ebony, depending on their origins in the anti-heavens.

28. Do dark angels possess light?

While dark angels do possess light, it is of lesser intensity compared to angels of light. Consequently, demons are not drawn to exceptionally radiant angels, as they risk being consumed by their brilliance. Instead, demons are attracted to dark angels due to their benevolence. We may liken this gentle darkness to a sanctified twilight, where darkness is warm and mild.

29. Can dark angels exhibit both goodness and malevolence?

Primarily, dark angels are known for their unwavering rectitude. They exhibit acute discernment, distinguishing between good and evil, truth and falsehood, with remarkable clarity. Some dark angels are chosen by God for less pleasant tasks. Dark angelic warriors are tasked with instigating and overseeing wars or escorting malevolent spirits to Hell. They serve as guardians of the Hells.

30. Can both light and dark angels incarnate on Earth?

Both light and dark angels share a common aspiration to experience earthly life in physical bodies. Therefore, they possess the capacity to incarnate on Earth.

31. How do angels manifest to humans?

Angels may appear as radiant spheres of light, capable of impressing even photographic paper. They can visit humans in dreams, deliver messages, or take on human form, appearing consciously before us. For instance, the angel of Joseph appeared in a dream, announcing the birth of Jesus. This same angel later guided Joseph in a dream, instructing him to flee to Egypt to protect the child from King Herod's persecution and indicating when it was safe to return to their homeland following Herod's death. The Virgin Mary also received a visitation from an angel in a dream, heralding the birth of the Son of God.

32. Is being an angel a role or a state of being?

Being an angel represents a state of being rather than a role, profession, or attribute. Angels are inherently what they are.

33. Can angels be simultaneously present in multiple locations?

Angels have the ability to exist in countless places simultaneously, transcending the limitations of time and space. They can open gateways to multiple dimensions simultaneously and perform diverse missions concurrently.

34. Do angels descend to Earth? Under what circumstances, why, and in what form?

Angels occasionally descend to Earth, acting on missions directed by God. These missions may involve revealing divine future plans, such as the Annunciation, or bestowing gifts and graces. Angels may manifest under various conditions as per God's will.

35. What is angelic energy?

Angelic energy encompasses the luminosity emitted by angels, characterized by a high-frequency light that varies depending on their celestial origins.

36. How can we connect with angelic energy?

We can establish a connection with angelic energy through prayer directed towards angels, invoking their presence, visualizing them, using symbols associated with their celestial origins, or through icons—depictions of angels and spiritual entities.

37. hat is the relationship between angels and icons?

The act of consecrating icons results in the descent of angels associated with the depicted figure (e.g., St. Dimitri, the angel—such as Archangel Michael, or the illustrated Mother). The icon's efficacy is conferred by the potency of the angel invoked during consecration and the spiritual entity it represents. Moreover, as time passes, its influence deepens through the devotion of those who offer their prayers before it.

38. Can humans pray to angels?

Individuals may seek the assistance of angels according to the angels' specialisation. Prayer may be directed to one's guardian angel for heightened protection or to other angels, each associated with specific attributes or functions, depending on one's desires.

39. Is it possible for us to craft our own images, either envisioned or seen by us, depicting angels, whether painted, sculpted, or produced through printing?

When one endeavours to create their own angelic imagery, there exists a potential for error, as even malevolent entities have the capacity to assume the guise of angels. Yet, when one genuinely 'sees' an angel, offers blessings, and invokes its presence, a malevolent impostor will retreat, providing a discerning indicator of genuine angelic presence.

40. Does an angel, when portrayed through painting, sculpture, or printing, convey spiritual significance, or does it remain a mere representation?

The degree of connection to the respective celestial entity is directly proportional to the fidelity with which an image, sculpture, or painting resembles an angel. Such manifestations serve as metaphysical portals, facilitating a connection with the specific angelic being in question. It is worth noting, however, that Byzantine artworks may deviate from this general principle.

41. Can an angel perceive our thoughts or the words spoken when we summon them?

Indeed, angels have the capacity to apprehend our thoughts when we forge a spiritual connection with them, as well as to comprehend our spoken words when we invoke their presence. The synergy of thought and speech amplifies this connection.

42. Is there a secret 'password' to authenticate the presence of a true angel?

Certainly, among the veritable 'passcodes' utilised in angelic authentication, the phrase 'Most Holy Mother of God, Virgin' serves as one such exemplar. Demons cannot speak these words.

43. Could the sensation of déjà vu be interpreted as a form of communication from angels?

Indubitably, there is a variant of déjà vu that correlates with premonitions conveyed by angels, although instances of déjà vu can also emanate from less benign sources. Nonetheless, in the broader sense, the sensation of déjà vu often results from recollections of past-life experiences. During slumber, we traverse diverse spiritual realms, including the Akashic Records, where glimpses of the future may be gleaned. Upon awakening, these memories persist, subsequently recognized as déjà vu.

44. Do angels necessitate spiritual gold for their own purposes?

Indeed, spiritual gold constitutes a requisite for all

spiritual entities. This ethereal currency can be bartered for spiritual endowments and empowerment, serving as a medium for manifesting desires, whether material or spiritual. Angels, too, require spiritual gold to acquire wisdom, courage, potency, and the ability to perceive the fabric of time and space.

45. In what manner can angels generate spiritual gold?

Angelic beings are capable of acquiring spiritual gold from individuals who possess it, thereby aiding them in materialising wealth and material benefits. Notably, the archangels Gabriel and Uriel are regarded as specialists in this endeavour.

46. Do angels inherently possess power?

Angelic entities do not inherently possess self-derived power; rather, they derive their potency from a universal source of celestial light. In the context of our Universe, this universal source of divine radiance forms the wellspring of their strength.

47. Do all angels within our Universe derive their luminescence and authority from a common source?

Our Universe exists in multiplicity, housing various celestial realms. Consequently, the universal source of divine light encompasses all systems of belief and religions that have arisen on our planet. This encompasses Judaism, Christianity, Islam, Buddhism, and every other system of belief, with each entity forging a connection to this source with varying degrees of proximity. Analogous to distinct floors in a building, each belief system draws its light and energy from the level it has aspired to on this spiritual hierarchy. Thus, every soul partakes in this spiritual continuum, irrespective of their religious or faith-based affiliations. This divergence, in part, defines the varying levels from which angels derive their power, light, and mission assignments.

48. What are the corporeal signs that manifest in the presence of an angel?

Diverse corporeal signs may emerge over time, aiding in their identification. These include sensations of skin tingling, the sudden appearance of goosebumps, often referred to as 'spiritual shivers,' an effect of angels' inherently higher vibrational frequencies compared to our earthly realm. A sneeze coinciding with an affirmation of truth, an internal warmth spreading outward—typical of Archangel Michael—familiar scents from inexplicable origins evoking special memories, ringing within the ears, a method through which angels communicate messages one is not yet ready to hear, but which the mind will decipher in due course, butterflies in the stomach without external provocation, serving as a signal for heightened attention to a forthcoming decision, and an overarching sense of serenity and clarity, signifying the guidance and support of a Divine spiritual presence.

49. What indicators suggest that one is welcomed by the angels of a new place they visit?

Upon initial entry into a novel locale, individuals are often greeted by signs conveyed by the entities associated with that place. Such encounters transpire not solely on the inaugural visit but persist each time one returns to the location. A profound connection with oneself, paired with an elevated sense of awareness, enables the perception of these manifestations. For example, in a foreign metropolis where past-life connections may exist, the initial individual encountered—be it a restaurant attendant or parking attendant—converses in one's native tongue, despite the individual's efforts to communicate in a universal language. Additionally, a sense of comfort, restful slumber, or serendipitous discoveries of currency may also denote these welcoming signs.

50. What are the signs that indicate you are not welcomed by the angels of a new place you visit?

In certain circumstances, entities, angels, or even dragons might oppose your presence in a particular place due to past transgressions across lifetimes. In such instances, it proves beneficial to gauge these parameters through dowsing or alternative methods before your arrival at the location. If these parameters prove unfavourable, it's advisable to seek forgiveness from both the place and its resident entities in advance. Indicators that the angels of a place have not welcomed you might manifest as a persistent week of rainfall during a seaside vacation, attempts to ascend a mountain via cable car thwarted by unrelenting winds or dense fog, a disappointing culinary experience at the city's most renowned restaurant, an unfortunate loss of funds within the subway system, or the discovery of subpar accommodations marred by uncleanliness and unpleasant odours.

51. What practical method can we use to benefit from the protection of angels in specific urgent situations in our daily life?

In cases where you find yourself confronted with a situation that precludes the performance of elaborate rituals or the luxury of extended prayers or meditations, a practical and general approach involves establishing a connection with the four distinguished archangels. The archangels, being the celestial triad closest to humanity and the natural world, consist of Michael, Gabriel, Raphael, and Uriel. In your mind's eye, visualise positioning Michael to your right, Gabriel to your left, Raphael directly ahead, and Uriel positioned behind you, with the divine presence of God transcending all. Notably, there exists an ancient Jewish prayer invoking these four great archangels while arranging them in this protective formation.

52. What do the numerical sequences or numerical codes of angels signify?

Among the most prevalent signs conveyed by angels are numerical sequences or codes, such as 111, 333, 777, 1234, and the like. Numbers constitute fundamental instruments employed by angels to establish communication with us. The potency and significance inherent in the repetition of whole numbers have persisted for centuries, tracing back to the era of the illustrious Greek philosopher Pythagoras. Pythagoras, distinguished not only for his profound contributions to the realm of mathematics and the formulation of unique quantitative solutions, held a belief that our reality materialises as a physical manifestation of the energetic resonance of numbers. Mathematics serves as the cornerstone of existence, extending its influence even into the spiritual domain, forging a profound nexus between angels and numerical patterns.

53. Where do these angelic numerical patterns manifest?

Angelic numerical patterns manifest in the most ordinary of locales: on telephone numbers, vehicle license plates (often accompanied by letters that together convey a complete message), timepieces, alarms, addresses, receipts, price tags, travel itineraries - in essence, virtually anywhere.

54. How can we incorporate these angelic numerical sequences into our daily lives?

In the market, one can find a plethora of writings that meticulously detail various numerical sequences, their respective meanings, and the methods for deciphering these numerical messages. Upon the receipt of a numerical message (for instance, encountering the sequence "444" repeatedly throughout the day), one may opt for a straightforward meditative practice. This aims to harmonise the vibrational frequencies inherent in the numerical sequence with one's own life.

As an illustration, if the aspiration is to invite greater abundance into one's existence, a deliberate focus on or depiction of numerous instances of the numeral "8" is recommended. Should the desire be to imbue this ritual with heightened potency, an invocation of Archangel Gabriel, the celestial bestower of gifts, can be undertaken.

55. Do these angelic numerical sequences convey uniform messages to everyone?

While angels provide guidance encompassing all facets of your life, it's crucial to recognise that while the core message may be universal, these celestial beings personalise their messages based upon your individuality. Thus, it necessitates your vigilant attention to the inner dialogue, your thoughts, somatic sensations, the images that emerge, and your emotional responses. It is through these very channels that your angels tailor their messages to resonate with your unique essence.

56. What are the energetic hues attributed to angels?

Angels possess the capacity to assume a myriad of colours

contingent upon the specific mission they undertake or the purpose for which they are invoked.

57. Is there a correlation between numerology and angels?

Indeed, an intricate association exists between the spiritual realm, numerical patterns, and the domain of mathematics. Consequently, each angel harbours a numerical facet inherent within their name.

58. Can angels prophesy future events?

With the divine permission of God, angels have the capacity to convey tidings regarding future events. This serves the purpose of rendering God's celestial design more comprehensible to the human intellect. For instance, one can cite the example of the angel who forewarned Lot of the impending destruction of Sodom, or the angel who conveyed to Elijah the arduous journey that lay ahead, coupled with the prophecy of Ahazia's demise.

59. Does a hierarchy exist among angels?

Angelic entities are categorically organised into distinct hierarchies, with each angel possessing a specialised function. Certain angels are positioned proximate to the throne of God, while others oversee the activities of their fellow angels and, by extension, the entire universe. Simultaneously, there exist angels designated for the transmission of messages to humanity, accompanying and safeguarding individuals in their earthly sojourn.

60. How does this angelic hierarchy parallel the hierarchy of divine beings?

The angelic hierarchy is expansive, extending from the guardian angel to include angels overseeing planets, galaxies, and beyond. One might envisage angels as akin to nested

Russian matryoshka dolls, with each larger doll encapsulating a smaller one, and so forth. Each angel, predicated upon their hierarchical level, embodies unique attributes. A guardian angel possesses specific attributes, while a planetary angel embodies distinct qualities, and similarly, an angel overseeing a galaxy manifests its individual attributes, and so on. This intricate hierarchy mirrors the structure of divine beings, with all encompassed within the domain of the Primordial Deity.

61. Can an angel concurrently hold multiple specialisations and roles, participating in several angelic orders simultaneously?

In accordance with the principle of "as above, so below, and as below, so above," the answer is unequivocally yes. A person can take on the roles of both a father and a husband, thereby assuming the mantle of a guardian angel in the celestial reflection. Simultaneously, they may ascend to the position of a nation's president, mirroring the archetype of an angelic principality. Moreover, they might find themselves in a military capacity, holding the rank of supreme commander over the armed forces of their land, reflecting the essence of an archangel. They can also be a devout member of the clergy engaged directly in the spiritual battle against the forces of darkness, embodying the attributes of an angel of power or dominion, and so forth.

Just as, by way of example, Gabriel is recognised as an archangel, he also encompasses the qualities of Virtue and Power/Lordship. Likewise, he can serve as the guardian angel for an exceptionally remarkable and distinguished spirit, one entrusted with a unique mission for the betterment of Earth.

62. How many kinds of radiant angels exist according to the celestial hierarchy?

Pseudo-Dionysius the Areopagite, an anonymous Christian scholar from the 5th century, meticulously delineated a total of nine angelic orders. These nine orders are meticulously organised into three celestial triads, which orbit in varying degrees of proximity around the divine presence of God. Each celestial order receives divine enlightenment commensurate with its inherent capabilities. The nine tiers, comprising spiritual beings of luminous essence, grouped into three classes, are as follows: The Supreme Order (those in immediate, unmediated communion with God, governing the entirety of Creation): Thrones, Seraphim, and Cherubim; The Intermediate Order (entrusted with the governance of the universe and the delicate equilibrium between opposing forces, such as good and evil, the celestial and the terrestrial): Dominions, Virtues, and Powers/Lords; and The Lower Order (tasked with orchestrating worldly and individual activities): Principalities/Beginners, Archangels, and Angels. Nevertheless, collectively, we commonly refer to them as angels.

63. Who are the Thrones?

Thrones are the celestial beings entrusted with the dispensation of God's divine judgment. They are often depicted as colossal, resplendent wheels adorned with innumerable eyes. Thrones are revered as celestial governors, responsible for preserving the delicate equilibrium between the realms of material existence and the ethereal, and between the forces of good and evil.

64. Who are the Seraphim?

Seraphim are the angels closest to the divine presence of

God, encircling His divine throne, often described as "serpents of fire." They are represented as beings with four faces and six wings. When they descend to the earthly realm, they assume a tall, slender human form.

65. Who are the Cherubim?

Cherubim are the custodians of celestial wisdom and bearers of profound knowledge pertaining to God. Hence, when one seeks enlightenment, it is fitting to establish a connection and invoke the presence of Cherubim. They are dispatched to the earthly domain on momentous missions, such as the expulsion of humanity from the paradisiacal confines of the Garden of Eden. Ancient art frequently portrays Cherubim as sphinx-like entities, adorned with wings and bearing human countenances.

66. Who are the Dominions?

Dominions receive divine mandates from the Seraphim and Cherubim, which they subsequently delegate to the other celestial entities—the celestial executors of these directives. As above, so below... Their primary objective is to ensure the preservation of cosmic order. To fulfil this divine mandate, they extend their influence to earthly leaders of nations, governments, and other authorities. Zadkiel holds preeminence among the Dominions. For those of us who bear the mantle of authority in our respective vocations, establishing a celestial connection with Zadkiel is imperative for guidance and empowerment.

67. Who are the Virtues?

The Virtues are entrusted with the sacred duty of upholding the natural equilibrium of the world. They provide guidance to humanity in domains closely associated with progress and development, including science, pioneering inventions, artistic endeavours, sports, and more. The Virtues manifest as radiant sparks of light. They receive their celestial directives from the higher echelons of celestial entities and, on occasion, transmute these directives into wonders and miracles for those deemed deserving. Thus, individuals engaged in diverse artistic realms (music, painting, theatre, etc.), as well as writers, physicists, chemists, IT specialists, and even athletes, are urged to seek the celestial guidance and benevolence of the Virtues.

68. Who are the Powers/Lords?

The Powers, also known as the Lords, serve as celestial intermediaries, positioned at the celestial threshold that bridges the chasm between Heaven and Earth. Among their celestial ranks, one encounters the angel of death. They perform the crucial role of negotiators, overseeing interactions with malevolent entities that harbour intentions of unleashing havoc upon the world. Furthermore, they serve as celestial guides in matters of religion, theology, and ideology. The Powers, or Lords, are often depicted as vividly hued yet somewhat nebulous, ethereal entities.

69. Who are the Principalities/Beginners?

The Principalities, or Beginners, stand as celestial overseers of every facet of earthly existence. They shoulder the responsibility of governing nations, cities, and localities, offering divine guidance in the organisation of human communities. No new nation or autonomous territory emerges without their celestial consent and divine guidance, graciously bestowed by God. The Principalities, or Beginners, assume the form of radiant rays of celestial light.

70. Who are the Archangels?

The Archangels, along with their celestial brethren, primarily serve as protectors of humanity and all corporeal entities. They constitute the inaugural celestial order that manifests exclusively in human form. Their celestial guidance proves indispensable to explorers, champions of human rights, philosophers, and those who traverse the realms of thought and inquiry. This celestial order finds the most frequent mention in the sacred texts of the Bible, particularly with reference to the Archangels Michael, Gabriel, and Raphael.

71. Who are the Angels in accordance with the celestial hierarchy?

The Angels stand as the true intermediaries between the celestial realm of God and humankind. These angels are not affiliated with particular nations but rather tend to the pragmatic aspects of human existence: they oversee homes, vehicles, daily sustenance, and the welfare of humanity. They provide nourishment, counsel, and healing—they are the celestial guardians.

72. How are the angels arranged in terms of micro and macro verses?

The celestial realms are arranged with an intricate design: Heavens within Heavens, nestled within Heavens, and further nested within Heavens. Each celestial sphere, in its own right, comprises ten celestial hierarchies, and within each of these celestial spheres, reside angels meticulously structured in hierarchies, akin to the celestial hierarchies elucidated by Pseudo-Dionysius the Areopagite—consisting of nine angelic orders, each meticulously organised into three triads.

73. What are guardian angels?

Guardian angels, in essence, epitomise the divine grace that God bestows upon an individual. Every human, regardless of their lineage, nationality, or creed, is endowed with a guardian angel from the very moment of birth. These guardian angels may vary in the magnitude of their celestial influence.

74. From whom do we receive our guardian angel?

It is imperative to distinguish the guardian angel from the angel of baptism. When a God dispatches us into the realm of corporeal existence, He assigns us a guardian angel, calibrated to His spiritual station. Consequently, this guardian angel may emanate from a celestial echelon either loftier or humbler than the baptismal angel.

75. How do I connect with my guardian angel?

The most straightforward avenue to establish communion with our guardian angel—or indeed, with any entity, be it God, a fellow soul, a sentient creature, or even a sacred site—is through the realm of thought. The mere act of contemplation, driven by the intention to forge a connection, inexorably binds us with our guardian angel.

76. How do I discern the identity of my guardian angel, facilitating a profound connection?

To unequivocally secure a connection with our guardian angel, we must first embark on a journey of acquaintance. Our guardian angel possesses a name, embodies a gender, which may also assume an androgynous nature, boasts an astral age, and exudes distinctive attributes, encompassing facets such as humour, intellect, and steadfastness. A preliminary step may encompass the practice of meditation, invoking the Reiki guardian angel meditation as a template, which can be seamlessly adapted to facilitate communion with one's guardian angel.

77. When is it expedient to engage in communion with our guardian angel?

The practice of sustained connection with our guardian angel proves propitious in perpetuity. There emerge moments when trepidation, anxiety, and heightened emotions inundate our senses, or when a yearning for augmented guidance surfaces. During these intervals, summoning the benevolent presence of the guardian angel proves invaluable. Consider, for instance, its utility when traversing the labyrinthine pathways of a job interview, confronting the crucible of an examination, undertaking a formidable mission, convening with a contentious interlocutor, or simply when an insatiable appetite for added protection beckons. The firmer the bond we cultivate with our guardian angel, the deeper our tether to the ethereal realm becomes, facilitating the seamless reception and profound comprehension of messages disseminated from realms unseen.

78. What underpins the quintessence of the relationship between a human being and their guardian angel?

The guardian angel harbours a personal mission, one anchored in the bedrock of nurturing, guiding, and safeguarding the individual under their celestial watch.

79. Can a guardian angel manipulate an individual to heed their counsel?

The guardian angel, while assuming the roles of vigilant custodian, protector, and sage guide, remains beholden to the sacred principle of honouring free will. However, as the guardian angel, too, possesses the sovereignty of free will, they might opt to sway the volition of their earthly charge, albeit in a benevolent and uplifting manner.

80. Can guardian angels fall in love?

Indeed, angels are susceptible to the stirrings of affection toward those placed under their ethereal stewardship or even toward others with whom they serendipitously cross paths. Should an angel's heart incline toward another soul, they may discreetly steer their "protege" toward that other individual, in order to express their celestial affections through them. Hence, this may engender the paradoxical phenomenon where the angel within an individual harbours love for another, while the individual's own self may remain oblivious or indifferent.

81. What fate befalls the guardian angel when a mortal breathes their last?

The guardian angel remains steadfastly at the side of their earthly ward until the moment of personal reckoning, a celestial tribunal convened forty days after the earthly demise.

82. What is the Guardian Angel's role during the 40 days?

Throughout these 40 days, the Guardian Angel leads the individual through every place and circumstance they have encountered, allowing them to perceive their life from a divine perspective and conduct a comprehensive analysis.

83. What transpires with the Guardian Angel during an individual's days of fasting and spiritual purification?

During these periods, the Guardian Angel becomes infused with light as it cleanses all of the individual's energy centres. This process amplifies the light passing through these centres, enhancing their luminosity and power.

84. At what juncture does the Guardian Angel make its presence known to a child?

The Guardian Angel arrives while cradling the soul of the individual, within which their spiritual mission, divine potential, and instructions from the level of God, the source of the soul, are inscribed. The Guardian Angel accompanies the child from the moment the mother perceives the movement during pregnancy, typically in the third or fourth month.

85. Is there an angel assigned to pregnant women and childbirth?

Indeed, there is an angel named Gabriel, who not only presides over the moment of conception but remains with the expectant mother until the onset of labor contractions.

86. Can the protection of a woman and her pregnancy be enhanced through a connection with Gabriel?

Yes, nurturing a stronger bond with Gabriel is possible through various means, including fasting, prayer, kindling candles consecrated to Gabriel, attending religious services, embarking on pilgrimages, and performing acts of kindness. This amplification elevates both the strength and protective capacity that Gabriel can offer to the mother and her pregnancy. Conversely, a weakening of Gabriel's power may diminish this safeguard.

87. Is there an archangel for mothers, fathers, and parents in general?

The archangel Gabriel, the same celestial entity associated with pregnancy and childbirth, extends his protective mantle over mothers, fathers, and families as a whole.

88. Do we choose our angels at birth, or do they choose us?

The assignment of a guardian angel occurs through resonance and divine decree, orchestrated by God. Rarely, and only from a certain spiritual vantage point in the individual's journey, can one consciously select their guardian angel or angels to fulfil a specific personal mission.

89. What happens to a child's guardian angel if the child frequently experiences accidents, injuries, or perilous situations and appears not to learn from past events?

In such instances, the guardian angel of the child may lack the sufficient power to protect them, or the negative energy directed toward the angel may exceed its capacity to withstand (including negative energies emanating from the child's parents). This may occur due to personal or ancestral karma or due to the loss of the child's soul for various reasons. The remedy lies in bolstering the power of the child's guardian angel.

90. Does the guardian angel guide from within or from outside?

While an individual remains asleep at the level of their inner self, the guardian angel serves as the inner guiding consciousness. Following spiritual awakening, the guardian angel manifests externally to offer guidance, and the individual, operating from the level of their inner self, guides their physical body. Even though communication transpires at the mental level, thus internally, after awakening, the guardian angel operates externally.

91. Can you enhance the personal power of your child's guardian angel?

Yes, you can increase the strength of your child's guardian angel through various methods. As a parent, you are allowed to pray on behalf of the guardian angel. As a daily practice to enhance your child's protection, you can light a white candle each evening, consecrating it to your child's guardian angel with gratitude for their safeguarding.

92. Is the presence of a guardian angel necessary if one can establish a connection with the Divine Self, a source of communication and divine guidance?

Indeed, it is. This necessity arises from the intricate balance inherent to the human condition, one that encompasses both the luminous and shadowy aspects of existence. Within the human vessel, manifestations originate from divine constructs, including the guardian angel, as well as from darker elements. The guardian angel assumes the pivotal role of enabling the corporeal manifestation of the human form. While the Divine essence permeates all, the guardian angel serves as the custodian of the body's well-being.

93. How does one respond when their guardian angel obstructs their spiritual evolution?

When a guardian angel impedes spiritual progression due to an allegiance to a deity who proclaims exclusivity as the sole path, it becomes imperative to transcend such hindrances. The duty of the seeker extends beyond servitude to a singular deity and aligns with the pursuit of ultimate truth—the Primordial Divinity.

94. What course of action is advisable when confronted with resistance from the guardian angel of a partner, spouse, child, or clergyman, hindering one's spiritual journey?

In the face of any angelic resistance impeding the pursuit of spiritual veracity, regardless of its motivation, individuals possess the prerogative, granted by the Primordial Divinity, to surmount such obstacles. One's allegiance is not confined to a solitary deity but converges with the paramount truth embodied by the Primordial Divinity.

95. Could you elucidate the concept of "deprogramming" a guardian angel and describe the process involved?

Certain angels adhere to beliefs that lack comprehensive veracity, such as the baptismal angel, whose convictions may align exclusively with Jesus, obstructing any doctrine contrary to Christian tenets. In such instances, one possesses the agency to prevail over these convictions and redirect these angels to higher celestial echelons, where they can refine their comprehension of truth. This transformative process is aptly termed "deprogramming."

96. How may angels be concealed within alternate dimensions, conditioned to safeguard against pilferage by external forces, and empowered to retain their celestial potency?

Indeed, angels are susceptible to appropriation by individuals possessing superior knowledge and spiritual stature. To mitigate this vulnerability, the most effective course of action entails the repositioning of these angels within higher celestial dimensions, wherein they remain impervious to theft. These celestial beings can be conditioned to provide assistance during critical junctures, accumulating power and luminance each time individuals engage in virtuous actions.

97. What happens to our guardian angel during psychic attacks on us?

Guardian angels suffer alongside us, as they are the first to be impacted during such attacks.

98. How may we facilitate the healing of our afflicted guardian angels?

The celestial guardian's well-being can be restored through an infusion of light, achievable through fervent prayer, rigorous fasting, the kindling of sacred flames, the harmonious resonance of high-vibrational melodies, sacred pilgrimages, participation in consecrated anointment ceremonies, the activation of Reiki's luminous conduits, and the collective support and shared luminosity of a community of kindred celestial beings. Such unity permits these celestial beings to recuperate and renew their luminous essence.

99. Until what juncture is it plausible to tend to the guardian angel of one's offspring?

The commitment to nurture and sustain the guardian angel remains unrestricted by temporal constraints. Regardless of age or circumstance, the guardian angel operates autonomously, perpetually dedicated to the safeguarding of its charge.

100. To which chakra does the guardian angel demonstrate the strongest affinity?

The guardian angel maintains its primary connection with the third chakra, which encompasses the sphere of protection, yet its ethereal tether extends to encompass all other chakras.

101. In cases of panic attacks, depression, or ailments—whether mental or physical—what fate befalls the guardian angel?

During such adversities, the guardian angel becomes besieged by malevolent energies targeting the afflicted individual. As a consequence, these dark energies may manifest physical or psychological afflictions.

102. Is it incumbent upon a spouse to attend to the guardian angel of their partner if they fail to do so?

Indeed. Through the union of marriage, they become one, with each partner capable of invoking the guardian angel of the other. Simultaneously, they can reciprocate and offer assistance in kind.

103. Why do certain priests or mentors abscond with the angels of those they initiate, and how might a pupil reclaim them?

Regrettably, there are mentors or priests unaware that during initiation, they may receive angels in parity with the ones received by the initiate. Appropriating another's angels is deemed a spiritual transgression, and the remedy is to emanate light to the pilfered angels for their restitution of potency and return.

104. Can a human beseech God for a more substantial guardian angel?

Affirmative. A plea for the substitution of one's guardian angel is admissible both for the supplicant and others. Should one deem their guardian angel feeble, unable to furnish ample protection, or discover that their guardian angel is beholden to a deity and, rather than aiding, impedes ascension to a loftier realm, such a supplication is permissible.

105. How can one attune to the presence of the guardian angel?

To sense the ethereal realm, and consequently the guardian angel, one must heighten sensitivity through prayer and fasting. The elimination of animal products from one's diet enhances sensitivity, elevates bodily vibrations, and inherently opposes conflicting vibrations.

106. When does the guardian angel conclude its mission with a spirit?

Initially, it was surmised that a guardian angel fulfils its mission upon the individual's personal judgment. Yet, it is now discerned that it may continue to watch over that individual through subsequent incarnations, even descending to incarnate and proffer aid, including within the material plane.

107. Can accrued spiritual wealth be exchanged for a more formidable guardian angel?

Certainly. Initiations, for instance, permit the reception of angels from a superior echelon compared to the initiate's access until the moment of initiation. This is contingent upon the maximum level accessible to the master bestowing the initiation. The exchange of spiritual wealth is permissible to secure a more substantial angel.

108. Can communion augment the guardian angel's potency?

Indeed. Communion encapsulates particles, energy, information, and spirit from the Christic Heaven, thereby amplifying the guardian angel's strength.

109. What diminishes an angel's power?

Defeat in battle, participation in human sexual acts, magical interventions, violation of divine law, disobedience, and errors all contribute to the waning of an angel's power.

110. What transpires with the guardian angel of a prematurely born child?

Premature births occur due to the substantial size of spirits, causing discomfort in the mother's womb and precipitating birth. Alternatively, an overwhelming negative energy stemming from their karma or family can bypass the guardian angel of the mother, Gabriel, or the child, inducing contractions.

111. What type of guardian angel do self-aware, awakened children possess?

In the case of children born with innate awareness, it is essentially a technicality. Depending on their origin from a lower vibrational plane and the weightiness of their karma, they may have a diminutive, feeble angel, potentially leading to conditions such as autism or pseudo-autism.

112. What type of guardian angel accompanies children conceived through artificial insemination?

The guardian angels of children conceived through artificial insemination or in vitro fertilisation originate from the echelons of the God of this planet.

113. What symbiosis exists between our guardian angel and our demons?

In essence, humanity is crafted with a guardian angel tasked with guiding a negative entity. This underscores the educational role played by these angels in guiding demons, serpents (S.K. = Kundalini serpent = the individual's self). Each person is a composite of both an angel and a demon. The angel serves as our consciousness, while the demon embodies the shadowy aspect within us.

114. What sets apart the guardian angel from our spiritual guide?

The guardian angel is the celestial entity bestowed upon us at birth by the hand of God. On the other hand, spiritual guides may be acquired throughout one's lifespan, whether professionally upon completing an academic pursuit, through initiations, or even by engaging in various sports. Such guides can take the form of angels, dragons, departed martial arts masters, or saints who persist as guides for a community (for example, Saint Arsenie Boca for Romania).

115. Can our guardian angel be prone to furnishing erroneous information?

Certainly. Each angel derives its information from its particular plane, resulting in a limited perspective. An angel from a higher plane perceives things differently than one hailing from a lower plane.

116. Is it conceivable for our guardian angel to opt against defending us?

Several circumstances might warrant this. The angel may be restrained by divine command (the moment God leaves an individual to their devices) or when confronted by a superior power, be it a demon, a human, or another angel. Alternatively, the angel might be powerless if the individual has transgressed and the angel's potency has waned.

117. Can our guardian angel elect to part ways with us?

Our guardian angel undertakes its mission with free will—to care for us. However, it retains the liberty to distance itself from us at any juncture. Yet, the term 'leaving' implies withdrawal rather than complete abandonment or the cessation of intervention.

118. For what reasons might a guardian angel decide to sever ties with an individual?

Instances may include sinning, making persistent mistakes, disregarding guidance entirely, or habitually opting for malevolence. In such cases, our guardian angel withdraws but refrains from total abandonment. It remains until our death but may choose not to intervene.

119. Can our angels opt to leave us in favour of others?

Our guardian angel remains tethered to us from birth to death and cannot abandon us for another individual. Nevertheless, other angels associated with our professions, the angels of our virtues, or those linked to specific initiations may choose to redirect their guidance elsewhere.

120. Can the locales we frequent influence our guardian angel?

Each visited place possesses a distinct vibrational quality. Prolonged exposure to light enhances our guardian angel's potency. Pilgrimages to locales of elevated vibration prove beneficial, as exposure to high-vibration areas automatically imbues our angel with light. Conversely, visits to low-vibration places may deplete its power.

121. What daily practices can we adopt to augment our guardian angel?

Actions such as lighting candles consecrated to our guardian angel, presenting gifts at the altar, participating in charitable deeds, undergoing initiations into the light, and arranging for daily liturgies at monasteries contribute to enhancing our guardian angel. A portion of this energy directly benefits our celestial custodian.

122. What we consume impacts our guardian angel?

Every action either heightens or diminishes the strength of our celestial guardian. The cleaner our dietary choices, the higher our vibrational frequency, thus fortifying our angelic protector. This effect is most potent through rigorous black fasting and the consumption of foods rich in essence, such as olives, grapes, mangoes, pure chocolate, and organic wine.

123. Does our initial thought or intuition originate from our guardian angel?

If our soul is untarnished, the first stirrings of thought are indeed the whisperings of our celestial guide. Conversely, when surrounded by negativity, seeking answers tends to yield pessimistic responses. Hence, it becomes imperative to ensure the purity of our souls through prayer, fasting, and spiritual cleansing before seeking guidance, assuring the authenticity of the first response from our guardian angel. Even in a state of incomplete purification, entering the alpha state of the brain renders us impervious to negative energies in our surroundings.

124. Is imagination a gift from angels?

No, imagination is an intrinsic human faculty, a characteristic specifically aligned with the Yin aspect of human nature. While creativity may be inspired by angels, it stands distinct from mere imagination.

125. Do guardian angels possess individual consciousness?

Guardian angels, akin to humans, exhibit a consciousness of their own, encompassing all human traits. However, their connection to the Source is far more profound, endowing them with a heightened discernment between good and evil.

126. Are our angels the embodiment of our inner light?

Our luminosity is a composite of our angelic guardians' radiance, the luminosity of our soul, an emanation of the God within us, and the radiance corresponding to our self at the fundamental level.

127. Does the guardian angel share the same character as the individual they guide and protect?

Quite the contrary, God assigns a guardian angel to facilitate the growth of spiritual qualities and capabilities in the individual. Therefore, the angel arrives endowed with superior qualities to those of the individual. The schism between the individual and their guardian angel becomes the crucible for spiritual evolution, as the individual naturally gravitates towards the qualities of their celestial guide. Consequently, achieving these qualities marks both individual and angelic evolution.

128. If an individual's spiritual evolution propels them to a higher vibrational realm, how does it impact their guardian angel?

An individual's ascent to a higher realm through spiritual evolution results in a corresponding augmentation of their guardian angel. The angel receives divine gifts, graces, wings, and enhanced inner power as a reward.

129. What transpires with an individual's guardian angel when they transition to a more expansive dimension?

At this juncture, the guardian angel remains diminutive, diminishing the divine protection and internal luminosity of the individual. Subsequently, the individual is compelled to assist their celestial companion in regaining stature and inner strength.

130. Can humans metamorphose into angels after death?

Indeed, only those who have surpassed a specific spiritual threshold can transition into angels, undertaking designated missions such as caring for individuals or families. However, the prevalent belief that young children or exceptionally virtuous individuals who pass away prematurely automatically transform into angels is not necessarily accurate. In some instances, these souls are even angelic spirits incarnate, sent with a concise and specific mission to purify the karma of a particular family before returning to their celestial abode, mission accomplished.

131. Why delve into discussions about fallen angels?

The exploration of fallen angels is imperative because they are kin to angels. Their inverted value system necessitates our guidance to impart the truth. This pursuit is rooted in God's love, who, in His benevolence, created a realm where they could experience the full spectrum of existence, comprehend Him, and ultimately embrace His love.

132. How might fallen angels find their way back to God?

The primary prerequisite for fallen angels is unwavering obedience and a gradual assimilation of virtues such as mercy, love, and faith—essentially embodying the full spectrum of angelic qualities.

133. Are there fallen angels who resist the desire to return to God?

Certainly, the majority of fallen angels are entangled with the material realm and its primal indulgences: sex, alcohol, smoking, drugs. They adamantly resist the call to return to God, actively opposing divine influence.

134. Is incarnation a compulsory step for fallen angels on their path back to God?

Incarnation isn't obligatory for fallen angels seeking reconciliation with God, but immersion in the material plane is imperative. Spirits can undergo profound experiences without assuming physical form. Fallen angels, through possession, can engage in material experiences without formal incarnation.

135. Is Earth the exclusive conduit for fallen angels to seek reconciliation with God?

No, there exist numerous planets harbouring life where the process of fallen angels returning to God takes various forms. The human form represents just one manifestation through which the divine undergoes the intricate journey of the Demon's return to God.

136. What links fallen angels to extraterrestrial beings?

Extraterrestrials serve as just one modality through which the heavens facilitate the re-education of fallen angels. All forms of extraterrestrial entities trace their origins back to the same primordial self, initially adopting the guise of the kundalini serpent.

137. What intertwines fallen angels with the Sons of God?

The Sons of God trace their lineage to fallen angels. During the cosmic genesis of planets, humans were fashioned as God-like entities. For example, figures like Adam and Eve bore a soul and spirit bestowed by God, yet the kundalini serpent derived from the specific planetary environment. Their conscious choice to be born of the Holy Spirit symbolised their commitment to fulfilling God's divine will.

138. What is the role of sexuality for the fallen angels?

It serves to free them from negative programs and energies, infusing those who aspire to return to Heaven with light and soul, or charging with negative energies those who seek to grow in malevolence.

139. What constitutes an optimal relationship for any spirit with a fallen angel?

Both angels and humans, irrespective of their celestial origins, stand as kin to the fallen angel—the demon. Father Galeriu expounded on the concept of extending love even to God's perceived adversary, the demon.

140. Do fallen angels possess a consciousness?

Yes, albeit with an inverted value system. Fallen angels exist at varying levels of consciousness, their essence fundamentally inverted.

141. What connects martial arts with the narrative of fallen angels?

Martial arts emerged as a conduit for discovering truth through physical conflict. Faced with the absence of a direct relationship with angels, the pursuit of educating the demon took precedence. Martial arts, as a form of education, instills morality and positive attitudes, fostering the development of virtues in practitioners and guiding the demon back towards the divine path.

142. How do the degrees in martial arts correlate with fallen angels?

Martial arts degrees symbolise dimensions of fallen angels and/or levels of the antichrist to which a practitioner can descend without negatively impacting behaviour. The higher the dan number, the more a master/practitioner can descend or master more demons.

143. In what ways can fallen angels be defeated?

Fallen angels can be overcome through various means: by employing light and love, adhering to truth, wielding the sword, practicing martial arts, or engaging in sexual acts.

144. Is it possible for fallen angels to carry out God's will?

Indeed, when fallen angels decide to return to God, they begin to fulfil God's will and aid individuals in regaining their light for the journey back. The essential condition, though not the sole one, is to align with God's will.

145. Can fallen angels possess high intelligence or a high IQ?

Fallen angels can indeed possess exceptional intelligence, yet unfortunately, their intellectual prowess is directed toward malevolence. Those that exhibit outstanding intelligence and power are referred to as malevolent arch-strategists. Overcoming such arch-strategists transfers their potential to the victor.

146. How do fallen angels amplify their power?

Fallen angels augment their power by deceiving individuals, leading them into error, and seizing their souls. Additionally, they can boost their power through the angels they subdue and by harnessing the strength of the demons under their influence.

147. Do fallen angels experience more significant suffering in spiritual evolution compared to incarnated angels?

Certain fallen angels who remained loyal to God do not bear as heavy a karmic burden in incarnation, unlike some incarnated angels who may have been overly zealous as guardian angels. Generally, fallen angels face a more extensive transformation process. The greater the flaws upon arrival, the more profound the suffering in the material realm, as the evolution of fallen angels on Earth unfolds through hardship.

148. What is the relationship between vices, drugs, alcohol, gambling, and fallen angels?

Vices establish connections with major demons, particularly arch-strategists of substantial dimensions. Once on this path, a binding connection forms with the respective demon, whose astral age and power are considerable, making it challenging for an individual to break free from its influence and potentially leading to chronic involvement.

149. Why do fallen angels choose to incarnate?

Fallen angels incarnate to comprehend the dichotomy between good and evil, reclaim their angelic status, and subsequently return to Heaven. Initially, fallen angels are born, typically the most potent among them, within the animal kingdom. As they progress through successive lives, they incarnate in human form.

150. Do fallen angels possess knowledge of their origins?

No. Fallen angels, like all other spirits at the time of incarnation, experience a state of forgetfulness and are unaware of their identity or origin.

151. Can fallen angels ascend to heaven without undergoing incarnation on Earth?

Yes, fallen angels, having fallen due to disobedience, can ascend to God without incarnation if they learn obedience, even in the spiritual realm.

152. What attributes do the parents of an incarnated fallen angel possess?

Parents with a child who is a fallen angel can be both incarnated angels and incarnated fallen angels; they bear the responsibility of educating that spirit.

153. How can fallen angels (devils) be transmuted into light?

Through prayer, fasting, sports or martial arts, and sex. This transformation occurs by transposing them into positive affirmations, converting evil into good, and falsehoods/ concepts or misguided ideas into truth.

154. Can fallen angels experience love?

When they begin to liberate themselves from negative programs (sado-masochism), fallen angels start to experience love, even profoundly, but it is a form of demonic love.

155. What professions do fallen angels pursue on Earth?

Any profession. They engage in a myriad of occupations, including serving as priests.

156. Are there initiations that establish a connection with the fallen angels?

Indeed, there exist certain initiations within the realms of martial arts or shamanic practices that are dedicated to spiritual evolution. However, it's important to acknowledge the existence of satanic rituals that advocate the veneration of fallen angels and demons.

157. How potent can fallen angels become?

There are fallen angels who can encompass our material and spiritual universe, originating from other universes.

158. Can fallen angels exercise dominion over humans?

Yes. One measure of an individual's power is the size and maximum number of demons they can control. After subduing them, the demons/fallen angels remain under their influence.

159. Can fallen angels be instrumental in acquiring wealth and material possessions?

Yes. Fallen angels are more closely connected to the material plane than angels, so to fulfil their needs through humans (alcohol, drugs, food, pleasures, entertainment), they guide people toward generating wealth. If directed towards negativity, they steer individuals toward scams, theft, fraud, etc. If they have started aligning with God's will, they engage in businesses that benefit everyone on a win-win basis.

160. Why can one sell the soul of a fallen angel?

Because the soul, or spiritual gold, serves as currency to obtain things or services, even in the spiritual realm. In hell, the possessor of spiritual gold is the master, while the one without becomes a slave.

161. From where does the soul of an incarnated fallen angel originate?

Incarnated demons can come from other universes, and in such cases, they receive their soul from the God of the Universe from which they originate. They can also receive a soul from the God of the planet Earth and the God of our Universe.

162. Do fallen angels still possess free will?

Indeed, they retain the continual choice to turn back to God and engage in benevolent deeds, yet their inclination predominantly leans toward malevolence.

163. How do fallen angels reveal themselves in the presence of saints?

In the proximity of saints, shrouded by the radiance emitted by the saints, fallen angels enact virtuous deeds, albeit under the misconception that they are perpetrating malevolence. Certain fallen angels, influenced by the sagacity of the saint, commence aligning with God's will as a means to return to Heaven.

164. What transpires with fallen angels in the vicinity of saints' relics?

The radiance undergoes polarisation around the relics of saints. Consequently, these relics function as a portal to the heavenly tier that the respective saint has attained. Automatically, a portal remains ajar. Certain fallen angels attempt to obstruct the emission of light (endeavouring to seal the portal), some are drawn towards the saint's luminosity, and some utilise the portal for their return to God.

165. What unfolds with fallen angels employing a saint's portal for their return to God?

The resurgence of fallen angels returning to God through that portal amplifies the potency of the saint, the locale, and the dimensional facets of the portal.

166. Do fallen angels participate in athletic activities? Is sports a conduit for their journey back to Heaven?

Certainly, through involvement in sports, fallen angels transmute obscurity into luminosity. Through rigorous training, they amass energy and strength. In competitive arenas, they can ascend to the echelons of science and art. Their championship status essentially signifies the zenith they have achieved in that sport, symbolising their alignment with God.

167. What correlation exists between emotional wounds and fallen angels?

Emotional wounds burgeoned contemporaneously with the fall of angels. This implies that fallen angels predominantly carry a specific type or multitude of wounds. Consequently, the particles, information, energy, and spirit encapsulated in an individual's emotional wounds consist of micro or macro fallen angels. They ARE CONSTITUTED from fallen angels! :-)

168. What is the nexus between fallen angels and God?

Fallen angels constitute those who resist the Divine will and engage in conflict against God. God does not seek this; rather, angels with free will opted to oppose Him. The entire framework of the material Universe was purposefully crafted by God to provide an arena for fallen angels to undergo and comprehend the dichotomy of good and evil, and to make the choice to return to Heaven.

169. Where are fallen angels situated?

They reside in realms of damnation, anti-verses, or find themselves confined within the material, in the earthly plane.

170. Can all fallen angels attain salvation?

According to the doctrine of Universal Salvation propounded by Origen, the material Universe will conclude its course when the ultimate demon returns to God.

171. In the reception of angels during initiations, does one also welcome fallen angels?

The answer hinges on the nature of the initiation. There are those that usher individuals into the light (accompanied by angels of light), while others initiate into darkness (accompanied by fallen angels/demons).

172. Can we imbue ourselves with fallen angels through water, air, and sustenance?

Indeed. Water, air, and sustenance are composed of both angels of light and fallen angels. The sole distinction lies in the proportion between them. In essence, there exist predominantly positive sources of nourishment (wine, beer, mango, certain fruits, and vegetables, etc.) and predominantly negative sources (meat, cola, coffee, alcohol, etc.).

173. What transpires with fallen angels during the sacrament of confession?

In the course of confession, by acknowledging their transgressions, fallen angels forfeit their dominion over the individual and their soul. Through acts of contrition, they can ransom the soul lost due to that particular transgression.

174. What occurs with fallen angels during prayers of absolution?

The prayers of absolution emancipate the fallen angels, severing the ties or strings connecting them to the individual. Concerning curses, these prayers either compel the fallen angels to depart if the priest's authority surpasses theirs, or if not, they seek retribution against either the priest or the individual, potentially resulting in demise.

175. What unfolds with fallen angels during the liturgy?

Throughout the liturgy, the heavens unfold, permitting those who desire, possess the requisite values, and are duty-bound to ascend to loftier dimensions.

176. What is the doctrinal stance of Christianity regarding fallen angels?

Regrettably, Christianity views the fallen angel, the demon, as eternally condemned, failing to comprehend accurately the divine plan for the education of the fallen angel. Consequently, the standpoint of Christianity is confrontational, focusing on combat against the demon rather than fostering enlightenment.

177. How does light exert its influence on fallen angels?

Fallen angels remain unfamiliar with light, love, peace, and warmth. Light, possessing a vibration marginally higher than theirs, aids in their development. Should the vibrational frequency exceed theirs, it burns them. Consequently, light of elevated vibrational frequency can be employed to vanquish them or, if introduced gradually, can be harnessed in their instruction and preparation for elevation to Heaven.

178. How does love impact the fallen angel?

The effect is contingent upon their developmental stage. At a lower level of vibration, love may provoke irritation and discomfort. However, beyond a specific threshold, love annihilates the negative programs fuelling their aggressiveness.

179. Can fallen angels obstruct a church or sacred site?

Certainly. There exist demons that descend from realms surpassing the Christic level, capable of impeding a church or sacred location.

180. What is the correlation between an individual's strength and the fallen angel?

An individual's power corresponds to the might of the greatest demon they have conquered. When one prevails over a demon, the dominion of that demon is reclaimed by the person, mirroring their inherent potential.

181. Can fallen angels wield influence over human creative endeavours such as music or composition?

Indeed, fallen angels possess the capability to sway and shape various artistic expressions, encompassing music genres like rock, cinematic works, literature, composition, and the broader spectrum of art. However, their influence stands in stark opposition to the creative endeavours inspired by angels.

182. To what extent does pride manifest in fallen angels?

Pride within fallen angels reaches its zenith, escalating with the magnitude of their power. This pride, a formidable obstacle, impedes their return to God, as it restrains them from embracing humility.

183. How do fallen angels respond to the illuminating force of Reiki?

The radiance of Reiki embodies diverse vibrational frequencies. Some levels of vibration serve to assist and purify fallen angels, while others, resonating at higher frequencies, prove to be searing. The light of Reiki shares intrinsic attributes with universal light, seamlessly integrated rather than standing apart.

184. Do fallen angels adhere to a hierarchical structure?

Certainly, fallen angels adhere to a hierarchical order mirroring that of angels, albeit in opposition.

185. Who currently presides over Hell among the fallen angels?

In the present era, Lucifer no longer holds dominion over Hell, as he traverses the path of return to God. The mantle of rulership has been assumed by other demons.

186. What characterises the relationship between fallen angels and the divine?

Their relationship with the divine is one of resentment, condemning God for their descent, harbouring intense hatred, and vehemently resisting His divine will, constituting an enduring opposition to the entire cosmic creation.

187. How do fallen angels interact with the animal kingdom?

All creatures within the animal kingdom derive their existence from fallen angels. These angels represent the budding consciousness and soul, infused with life from the deity presiding over the Earth or the divine source from which they originate, recognizing the diversity of planetary origins for Earth's fauna.

188. What role do fallen angels play in shaping the elements—water, air, earth, fire, wood, and metal?

Fallen angels are intrinsic to the composition of all elemental forces on Earth, including water, air, earth, fire, wood, and metal.

189. Do fallen angels have distinct genders?

Certainly. Fallen angels embody both masculine and feminine qualities, appearing as incubi and succubi.

190. Which dance form among fallen angels is considered closer to divinity?

Fallen angels resonate with various dance forms based on their individual spiritual values. Whether expressed through rock or the swirling motions of dervishes, their affinity for dance varies.

191. Can a fallen angel undergo Reiki initiation?

Indeed. Through initiation conducted on a subtle plane, fallen angels may find a pathway to return to God. This involves implementing symbols that activate their structures and open dimensions towards the divine light.

192. Is it imperative for a fallen angel to achieve championship status?

Absolutely. Fallen angels, upon attaining championship through rigorous training, not only augment their power but also transmute darkness into light. Victory in competition allows them to absorb the essence and power of those they overcome, receiving accolades from the angel of victory when the heavens open on the podium.

193. Do fallen angels perpetually deceive, or can they speak the truth?

Fallen angels possess the duality to both deceive and speak the truth. In spiritual disputes, their testimony is heard by the divine judge and God. Unlike angels of light, fallen angels can articulate negative aspects about a person or situation, while angels of light typically function as informants.

194. Does an image of a fallen angel, be it a photograph or sculpture, hold spiritual power?

Undoubtedly. The spiritual potency of an image of a fallen angel intensifies with elements closely resembling the respective entity—whether in shape, colour, attributes, weapons, stars, or larger dimensions—establishing a stronger connection and amplifying its spiritual influence.

195. Can a fallen angel inflict harm, and do they possess weapons?

Yes, fallen angels wield an array of weapons, including forks, swords, ninja-like tools, whips, spears, axes, iatagane, and more. They have the capacity to inflict harm and derive satisfaction from the suffering of individuals, contingent upon their level of consciousness.

196. Can a fallen angel perceive you when invoked?

Fallen angels possess the ability to access and perceive your thoughts, voice, and intentions when granted permission. If positioned above you, they can have access without your explicit consent.

197. Why engage in combat or vanquish a fallen angel?

Engaging in combat or vanquishing a fallen angel may be necessary because it can inadvertently assail you, obstruct your endeavours, induce harm to others, compelling you to intervene. They possess the ability to disrupt devices, instruments, obliterate objects, provoke accidents, and oppose goodness.

198. What empowers a fallen angel during an attack?

Typically, the power of a fallen angel stems from your own vulnerabilities, defects, and wounds. It amplifies your personal wounds, defects, misunderstandings, frustrations, and fears.

199. How can you augment your potency in the struggle against fallen angels?

Potency in the battle against fallen angels emanates from self-level power, soul-level power, and consciousness-level power.

200. What transpires to vanquished fallen angels?

They metamorphose into your angels, and their power becomes yours, necessitating their submission. Furthermore, they embark on their spiritual evolution alongside you; they are in a state of learning.

201. Can fallen angels be educated?

Indeed. Once you comprehend facets of the spiritual and material realms, they too attain understanding.

202. Do you possess the right to engage in combat with fallen angels at any time?

In the event of an attack, you can engage in combat at any time. However, pursuing them without God's will is not permissible. The ability to conquer the demon is contingent on black fasting and prayer.

203. Is a fallen angel permitted to attack/strike me with God's approval?

Certainly. Instances exist where the assault of a fallen angel is sanctioned and willed by God: as a lesson, as a form of karmic retribution, as a restraint, as punishment, and so forth.

204. Does evolution occur in the confrontation with the fallen angel?

Yes. If you acquire its power, you automatically acquire its potential mirrored within, stripping away characteristics, power, and qualities, all leading to your evolution.

205. What must a fallen angel do to return to Heaven?

To aspire to return, to heed God's guidance, to comprehend the concepts of good and evil, to attain wisdom, humility, elevate vibration and inner light, and liberate itself from impediments and negative programs.

206. What is the foremost unconditional quality a fallen angel needs to regain entry to God?

Obedience.

207. What is the predominant lesson in our world?

Obedience. To parents, grandparents, educators, teachers, lovers, employers, bosses, the law, doctors, priests, masters, gurus, and, above all, to God.

208. How do fallen angels forfeit their power?

They lose their power when defeated, and through sexual encounters.

209. Are there foods that gratify fallen angels?

Meat, animal products, bitterness, spiciness, sourness... generally, intense flavours.

210. Can fallen angels achieve enlightenment?

Certainly. By amassing sufficient spiritual gold to generate their own light.

211. Do fallen angels possess inherent power, or do they derive it from elsewhere?

While they inherently possess power, they can also draw it from various sources: the people they parasitise, greater demons to whom they submit, through consumables, sexual activities, and from the angels they overpower, the saints they surpass, and even the gods they conquer.

212. Do fallen angels specialise?

They embrace all the specialisations of angels of light, but fallen angels work against God's plan, aiming to dismantle what angels construct.

213. What dimensions do fallen angels encompass?

From micro to macro. Similar to micro-macro dimensions in material realms, fallen angels span micro-macro ranges.

214. What constitutes fallen angels?

They are comprised of the particle of God from the Holy Spirit, albeit with altered information.

215. Are exorcisms of fallen angels appropriate?

Under specific circumstances, when demons are dispatched by humans or arrive without God's consent, exorcism is permissible.

216. Who assumes the role of guardian angels of karma?

Guardian angels of karma are embodied by demons. They are entities tasked with reinstating balance, ensuring individuals settle all debts owed to others. Why them? Because they lack mercy. Ponder the ordeal of Jesus; tormented by the guardian angels of karma to settle humanity's debts, they exhibited no mercy.

217. What is the relationship between the guardian angels of karma and the divine entitlement of humans?

Envision an individual without the right to possess wealth. Circling around such an individual are entities, the guardian angels of karma, diligently ensuring that he remains devoid of financial means, irrespective of his endeavours to attain it. Even if he accumulates more, these entities orchestrate circumstances where he loses that surplus—be it through a car accident, an unforeseen dental intervention, or the misplacement of his wallet. Should a person lack the entitlement to experience love or financial prosperity, any attempt on your part to bestow such blessings upon him results in you bearing the brunt of his karmic burden.

For instance, when a gentleman is devoid of the right to embrace love or physical affection, surrounding him are entities—guardian angels. If, out of compassion or love, you engage romantically with the gentleman, you inadvertently shoulder a portion of his karma. Thus, the assumption of karma extends to interpersonal relationships, manifesting when one loves someone against the preordained plan, marries against divine prescription, or engages in intimacy at an inopportune time, giving rise to offspring not descended from a lofty celestial realm and thereby diminishing one's divine entitlement.

218. Is there an angel attending to individuals at the moment of death, during the transition between worlds?

Seventy-two hours prior to an individual's demise, the angel of death approaches, supplanting the regular guardian angel, standing vigil to the person's right. The primary role of the angel of death is to facilitate the opening of the gateway, allowing the spirit to traverse from the material to the spiritual realm.

219. Can the angel of death be dispatched by someone other than God?

Indeed, in contemporary times, certain learned institutions comprehend the role of the angel of death and have acquired the knowledge to dispatch it to others.

220. What course of action is appropriate when the angel of death arrives, dispatched by someone other than God?

Upon its arrival, one may inquire, "Were you sent by God or another entity?" If the response is negative, one is permitted to prevail over it. Reference the narrative of Ivan Turbincă.

221. What if the angel of death arrives, sent by God?

Should it be dispatched by the primordial God, acceptance of one's departure is the only recourse. However, if one believes their mission is incomplete, prayers and requests for an extension of their personal mission are permissible.

222. Can negotiations transpire with the angel of death?

No, as it is a celestial emissary sent by God. Prevailing over it is the only option if dispatched by an external entity.

223. Can the angel of death depart without claiming the soul it came for?

Affirmative, if close relatives—spouse, parents, and children—petition on behalf of the person in question.

224. What is the correlation between angels and dragons?

Dragons are fallen angels, leaders, and superiors. Where a substantial dragon is present, a commensurate angel accompanies it. In the instance of a benevolent dragon of considerable size, a corresponding angel is in attendance.

225. What connection exists between angels and ascended masters?

Ascended masters are entities—be they fallen or incarnate angels—who have ascended to higher celestial realms. Having settled their karmic debts and severed ties with Earth, they achieve liberation. These entities may be situated either in realms beneath those of Jesus or above the heavenly plane associated with Christ.

226. What role do angels play in connection with the elements?

Angels of the elements exist, representing air, water, fire, Earth, and others. Each material element corresponds to a specific angel. Material substance is essentially condensed negative energy. Angels of the Earth element, for instance, possess the divine authority to transmute negative energy into the form of Earth. This principle extends to angels presiding over other elements.

227. What angels govern the elements?

The four primary elements—air, fire, water, and earth—are presided over by four significant archangels: Raphael, the archangel of air; Michael, the archangel of fire; Gabriel, the archangel of water; and Uriel, the archangel of earth.

228. Do angels oversee the cardinal points?

In certain passages of the Bible and Torah, God mentions the four winds of heaven or four directions, giving rise to the concept of archangels governing the four cardinal points of the Earth—namely, Uriel in the north, Michael in the south, Raphael in the east, and Gabriel in the west. To enhance the protection of our homes or workspaces, one can place statues or images of the archangels in the four cardinal points of the house or office with the intention of safeguarding the space.

229. Is there an angel for each month of the year?

Older Christian beliefs posit that just as each person has a guardian angel, every month of the year is overseen by an angel: January by Gabriel, or the Messenger; February by Barchiel, or the Angel of Compassion; March by Machidiel, or the Angel of Courage; April by Asmodel, or the Angel of Patience; May by Ambriel, or the Angel of Words; June by Muriel, or the Angel of Emotions; July by Vechiel, or the Angel of Affection; August by Hamaliel, or the Angel of Reason; September by Uriel, or the Angel of Inspiration; October by Barbiel, or the Angel of Sincerity; November by Adnachiel, or the Angel of Freedom; and December by Anael, or the Angel of Love.

230. What are the specialisations of angels?

Angels reflect certain aspects of divinity and, consequently, of humanity—what is above is also below. They specialise in different domains, various essential aspects of life, and can be invoked based on our needs. For example:

the angel of joy, wisdom, compassion, creativity, knowledge, discernment, harmony, abundance, etc.

231. Do angels take exams?

Yes, angels experience through humans. They attend a virtual school on Earth, learning virtually, while demons learn in the physical realm. Subsequently, they are usually born once to experience the physical and then demonstrate what they have learned, akin to a licensure examination. Theoretically, they may have only one life when they incarnate, but misunderstandings may lead them to linger in the earthly realm.

232. Is there a connection between money and angels?

There are two ways to acquire money: through angels (white money) or through demons (black money). Money is an energy, and like spiritual gold, it is coordinated by God through the agency of angels of gifts.

233. How can angels help with obtaining money?

Angels, the guides of gifts, we can possess them, receive them, lose them, or increase and decrease their power, depending on our actions. We can even increase our divine right in money through angels.

234. Can angels assist us in obtaining gifts and graces?

Yes, the angel of gifts is Gabriel, but not only him. By engaging in positive and unconditional actions for others each day, you aid and indebted yourself to God. At some point, an angel of gifts and graces arrives, and you are free to express and request the gift or grace you desire: wisdom, the gift of writing, the gift of singing, etc.

235. How do we know if we are manifesting the angel or demon within us?

Most often, individuals identify with their angel, their conscience. When you begin to act and identify at the level of self-awareness, you detach from your angel and begin to act as yourself. The meaning of life is human education. What religions misconceive is the identification of humans with their guardian angel. Man is the evil within us, and the angel is the one who educates man (i.e., the self of man, the S.K.).

236. What is the connection between angels and plant therapy, magic, spells?

According to Patriarch Enoch, Azazel taught magic and revealed eternal secrets known only to angels. Subsequently, Azazel and the angels subordinate to him disclosed secrets to other Earthlings, even consorting with Earthly women. As punishment, Azazel was bound by higher angels, cast out, and imprisoned in the desert until the Day of Judgment.

237. What is the connection between angels and the art of cosmetics?

In the era of Azazel, drawn to Earthly women, angels imparted upon them the skill of cosmetics, the craft of manipulating demons through incantations, and the intricacies of warfare. For breaching the codes of angels and unveiling the secrets of Earth, a punitive measure was exacted—stripped of their radiance, they metamorphosed into ebony fallen angels and were cast down to Earth.

238. Is there a nexus between angels and Earthly love?

Earthly love is a divine bestowment upon humanity and is channeled through Gabriel, the angel of endowments. He orchestrates encounters between two individuals and stands witness until a profound soul-level connection is forged between them. It is only God who discerns the identity of the person capable of reciprocating love, and through Gabriel, He orchestrates the rendezvous.

239. Is there an angel specialised in decisions concerning love?

Uriel is acclaimed as the sagacious one among angels, the repository of answers, especially when confronted with onerous decisions concerning an ideal romantic partner or the dilemma of persisting in a relationship.

240. What is the correlation between human emotions and angels?

Positive human emotions find their celestial guardians in angels. There exists an angel presiding over joy, an entity that tends to the care of happiness. Happiness, akin to any other affirmative emotion, is a divine gift and assumes the form of an angel. Attainment of happiness through angels is contingent upon deserving it. True happiness can only be found in God. It resides nowhere else. Once embraced by the angel of happiness, its sustenance is impervious to external factors—wealth, possessions, or the people surrounding us.

241. Do plants and animals possess guardian angels?

Every living entity in the material realm has a guide, a spirit that steers its existence and confers upon it a distinctive form. Just as a lion is directed by its entity to pursue an antelope for the perpetuation of its species, an antelope has its own guiding entity to navigate it away from a lion. Similarly, every plant has entities, spirits that nurture and care for them.

242. Who is the archangel of nature?

Entities—the angels overseeing the elements in nature, encompassing plants, animals, water, wind, and fire—are under the watchful gaze of Archangel Ariel. Ariel is occasionally depicted in a masculine or feminine guise, sometimes cradling a globe symbolising Earth or adorned with elements of nature, emblematic of Ariel's responsibility in overseeing God's creation on Earth. Ariel presides over the safeguarding, growth, and healing of animals and plants, as well as the stewardship of Earth's elemental components (water, rocks, wind, fire). Punishing those who harm God's creation, Ariel participated alongside God and the planet Earth in its creation.

243. Are there guardian angels of specific locales?

Every place, space, or element within a space is accompanied by an angel, a guide, a spirit. Thus, when one approaches the sea, it is propitious to offer a salutation and request permission from the angel of the water for a favourable reception. Similarly, when extracting a stone from a river or mountain, seeking consent from the spirit of that stone is considered a respectful act.

244. Are there angels dedicated to the act of healing?

Indeed, but not all angels possess the attribute and capability of healing. Healing angels manifested at the Pool of Bethesda, adjacent to the Sheep Gate in Jerusalem, where a multitude of infirm, blind, lame, and withered individuals awaited the stirring of the water. Periodically, an angel descended from heaven, agitating the water, and the initial person to immerse themselves post-disturbance was cured of any ailment.

245. Can angels also exhibit warrior-like characteristics?

God never yearns for warfare, but there are occasions when it becomes inevitable due to His dual nature of benevolence and justice. Consequently, warrior angels, tasked with executing God's plan, descend. Throughout history, there were commanders of modest armies who wielded swords of colossal proportions with seemingly effortless dexterity (as exemplified by Stephen the Great). This phenomenon could only be ascribed to the presence of warrior angels descending upon them, akin to the archangel Michael.

246. Can we alter the purpose of an angel, transforming a healing angel into a warrior angel or vice versa?

No, such a modification is beyond our purview as humans. The mission of angels is exclusively ordained by God or achieved through incarnation.

247. Can we acquire additional angels throughout our lives, beyond the guardian angel?

Certainly. While the guardian angel is a constant companion from birth, there are various moments in life when additional angels are bestowed upon us. These occasions include events like baptism, marriage, when assuming the role of a godparent at a wedding or baptism, monastic tonsure, ordination, and instances when the heavens open, allowing angelic hosts to descend. Furthermore, angels can be gained through Reiki initiations, neo-Reiki, any spiritual system of light, or even by undertaking extended periods of black fasting.

248. Is there a disparity in the potency of an angel within a monastery compared to that of a church or chapel?

Indeed. The strength of angels in a monastery is typically

more profound because monks or nuns, who have devoted their lives to God, reside, fast, and engage in prayer there. The influence of a place is determined by the number of priests, monks, and parishioners who frequent it and engage in prayer. The frequency of services, the abundance of lit candles, fervent prayers, and the possession of relics of saints all contribute to the augmented power of a monastery or church.

249. During Christian services, can angels from other realms descend and partake?

Certainly, during Christian services, the heavens can unfold beyond the Christic level if the priest is an incarnated angel from above the Christic level. Consequently, angels from higher and lower dimensions may participate.

250. How did angels contribute to the dissemination of Reiki, and which angels were involved?

The angel through whom Reiki emanated is Uriel. Initiations and the opening of Heaven facilitated the descent of angels from Uriel's level. The efficacy of angels at Uriel's level played a pivotal role in the widespread adoption of Reiki. Additionally, the fact that Reiki was offered to all humans without hierarchical constraints further propelled its dissemination.

251. Why are the angels received through Reiki initiations, etc., significant?

Each system into which we are initiated introduces angels from a specific spiritual level. Starting with Reiki and subsequent neo-Reiki systems, these systems access higher dimensions, allowing initiates to tap into the information and energy from those realms.

252. Does our personal power increase with the number of angels we have?

Yes, both the number and strength of our angels are crucial. In our journey, it is imperative to enhance both wisdom and power. A portion of our strength stems from the number and potency of our angels.

253. Can angels violate our free will?

Guardian angels meticulously respect our will. They patiently await our request for assistance, intervening in our lives only with divine permission. However, angels, in general, may overlook the free will of humans or angels under their hierarchy to fulfill their personal missions, irrespective of the desires or needs of others.

254. Do children have angels?

In addition to the guardian angel, children can have other angels. These angels can be obtained or have their power increased by parents through their actions, dedicating their positive deeds to the angels of their children. If a child is baptised, they also receive a baptismal angel. Parents can pray or light candles daily for the angels of their children to increase their power for protection and guidance. All angels received later in life will still be under the guardian angel.

255. How can we enhance our qualities through angels?

Even if we weren't born with many qualities, talents, or gifts, we can obtain them through our guardian angel by enhancing their qualities and power. Alternatively, we can acquire specialised angels in domains we desire.

256. Is man loved by God more than angels?

Because humans have the capacity to perform deeds

more special than angels, possessing the consciousness of good and evil, which angels lack, humans can pleasantly surprise God. Yes, God may indeed love humans more in such instances.

257. Is there a sense of jealousy among angels toward humanity?

Indeed, there exists a sentiment of jealousy, an envy within angels toward humans, for humans possess the capacity to experience both the benevolent and malevolent aspects of the material realm and life in its entirety.

258. Can humans engage in combat with angels? Can a confrontation occur between them on equal grounds?

Certainly, yes. Consider Morihei Ueshiba, the progenitor of Aikido, who engaged in a three-day battle with an angel named Ameno Kami. Subsequent to prevailing over the celestial being, he laid the groundwork for a novel martial arts discipline, assimilating insights gained from the angel.

259. Can angels be disheartened by humans?

Angels experience a sense of dismay when humans deviate from their guidance and commit errors. Each misguided action of a human detracts from the angel's potency, potential, and luminosity, akin to how virtuous deeds of a human contribute to the growth of the celestial entity.

260. Can angels harbour animosity and seek retribution?

Angels, akin to humans, exhibit comparable traits — they can be incensed, harbour animosity, seek retribution, withdraw, etc. Notwithstanding, angels lack the innate ability to forgive; this is a lesson they need to acquire.

261. Can angels deliberately inflict harm?

Angels can employ a luminous sword, bind, cast enchantments, and manipulate circumstances in a manner they perceive as conducive to benevolence.

262. Can angels be subservient to a human? Under what circumstances?

Angels may assume a subservient role through initiations, particularly when a human prevails over them in combat or garners their respect. Notably, certain individuals, such as saints or specialised priests, witness angels descending and joining in their divine service. Such remarkable individuals, characterised by exceptional goodness, purity, and wisdom, command the attention of angels.

263. Can angels be bestowed upon deceased individuals through initiations?

Indeed, such bestowal is feasible, as initiations transpire on the astral plane and are enacted with the consent of the departed souls and the divine will. This process serves as a means for ascending into the light or surmounting specific spiritual thresholds.

264. What offerings can be presented to angels in gratitude for their assistance?

Angels appreciate offerings of a beneficent nature — candied fruits, pistachios, almonds, fresh fruits, pastries, and similar tokens. By dedicating these offerings to others or providing alms while consecrating them to the angels, one aligns with their preferences.

265. How can we enlist the aid of angels in the realm of sports?

Angels, by their nature, aren't crafted for athletic pursuits, but they can assist us in post-sport recovery, in recuperation, healing, discovering nourishing foods, optimal supplements and vitamins, and in identifying the right coach or training facility, among other aspects.

266. Do angels oversee the domain of football?

Indeed, there are specialised angels for every sport. Football, in particular, is overseen by angels from realms above the Christic level, submitting to a God greater than the Christic deity. In general, team sports draw guidance from elevated spiritual echelons, with the size of the team correlating to a higher spiritual tier.

267. What is the intricate connection between angels, football, and the divine?

Football, as a sporting endeavour, emerged through a divine force that, via football, gathers souls. Within teams—be it players, coaches, or staff—coordinating angels exist. Alongside supporters, they emotionally fortify, channeling their souls into the football team. The adage holds that the audience acts as the 12th player. In the event of a loss, the soul partly returns to the victorious team and partly to the God of football.

268. Who embodies the role of the angel of victory, and what attributes characterise this celestial being?

The angel of victory is the ethereal entity that crowns individuals or entire teams with the laurel of triumph. This laurel can manifest both in human struggles against demons and in sporting competitions. In the realm of sports, when an individual or a team emerges triumphant, the angel of victory descends, bestowing light, gifts, graces, and potentials upon the winners. Those with a discerning eye might witness, during award ceremonies, the heavens opening above the podium. The essence is that in any competition, whether in sports, arts, sciences, or any field, the victor or victors receive a crown delivered by the angel of victory. This crown's energy is transcribed at a genetic level and is transmitted, including to descendants. Therefore, in canine or equestrian competitions, people seek descendants of champions because they inherently carry the notion of victory in their genes.

269. Is it crucial for a guardian angel to guide someone toward becoming a champion?

Certainly, as anything acquired by an individual when becoming a champion—through effort, work, and training, be it light, gifts, or graces—reflects back on the guiding guardian angel. This dynamic also extends to the coach and the coach's angel.

270. How does the demeanour of guardian angels change concerning individuals who ascend to champion status?

Guardian angels perceive the laurels attained by individuals upon becoming champions, earning them the respect of the angels. After achieving champion status, individuals receive even more guidance from their guardian angels. If someone attains champion status without deserving it, not only do they fail to receive graces and laurels, but the angels are aware of this and do not hold them in high regard.

271. How can angels be integrated into the realm of art?

Art, in its essence, is an expression of grace, whether innate or attainable through angels. Angels can be harnessed across various artistic fields based on their inherent specialisation. In this pursuit, one may implore God to dispatch angels to aid in the fulfilment of personal artistic missions.

272. In what ways can angels be instrumental in business?

Prosperous enterprises are steered by the angel of gifts. Angels of wealth guide individuals toward thriving businesses, opportune ventures, and optimal collaborators across various domains.

273. How do angels operate during a medical procedure or surgery?

The structure of medical procedures aligns doctors with the right side of patients, symbolising the position of the guardian angel. Hospitals, typically, are erected on sites inhabited by healing angels and dragons. Healing angels manifest within hospitals, guided by healthcare professionals. Doctors, nurses, and healthcare workers receive angels associated with their profession through education, which manifests through them in the hospital setting. In a medical procedure, the patient has their angel, the medical staff has their angel, the location has its angel, and in operating rooms, portals may open, allowing angels from higher dimensions, specialists in healing, to intervene as per divine will to save the respective patient.

274. How can the support offered by angels during a medical procedure or surgery be intensified?

Amplifying angelic assistance can be achieved through prayers from healthcare professionals, the prayers of family members and loved ones, the lighting of candles, the projection of the souls of loved ones onto the patient in the waiting room, sending light to the angels of medical professionals and the location, and invoking angels through Reiki. Techniques such as energizing and amplifying energy fields, restructuring structures, and the soul using dowsing techniques, among others, can also be employed.

275. How do angels assist us in our journeys?

Angels aid us in selecting the optimal and beneficial path to reach our desired destination, shielding us from potential accidents. For instance, if we feel we have taken an incorrect highway exit, our travel angel and guardian redirect us from something more adverse. They may offer guidance on halting at an optimal location where we might find excellent food, encounter special individuals, or discover significant benefits. It is imperative to be consciously aware that we are under the guidance of our travel angel and to heed their counsel.

Uriel, the specialised angel of journeys, establishes a beneficial personal relationship. Invoking him prior to commencing a journey, or carrying an icon or amulet bearing his representation, enables him to manifest and protect us effectively.

276. Is there an interconnection among all angels?

On the principle of oneness, indeed. All angels are interconnected through the unified field, a connection rooted in the divine. Therefore, the angel overseeing our journey comprehends precisely how to guide us—where to proceed, where to pause, what to explore—in harmony with other angels and aligned with our predetermined goals and objectives.

277. Can angels block our paths?

Certainly, angels can impede our progress in accordance with the divine will and for various reasons. They might divert us onto the optimal path, steering us away from a potential accident, a guidance that doesn't infringe upon free will but directs us. They may obstruct our path to give rise to synchronicities or hinder us temporarily (e.g., if we misplace our keys), averting potential issues had we arrived on time. Alternatively, they might block our way as a gentle reminder of their presence.

278. Do angels have a penchant for food?

Lacking physical bodies, angels do not require sustenance. However, certain references in the Bible allude to angels possibly "partaking in heavenly food sweet as honey." Angels can experience the essence of food through the medium of humans.

279. Are there specific foods that angels favour?

Indeed, angels exhibit a fondness for sweets and fruits.

280. How can one discern if angels respond to desires, requests, or prayers?

Should one make a specific request or find oneself uncertain in a particular situation, an observant individual might notice that within a brief timeframe, three distinct persons introduce the topic of Reiki therapies, for instance.

281. Can we invoke angels even if we aren't baptised Christians?

While the Bible references archangels such as Gabriel, Michael, Uriel, Raphael, and others, this does not confine them exclusively to Christianity. For instance, Gabriel is also recognised as the angel of revelation in the Quran, a figure frequently mentioned in Islamic scripture. Muslims, when reciting the Quran, invoke Gabriel.

282. Do angels remain present during intimate moments?

Angel Gabriel is present during the procreative act, when the future parents engage in intimate activities. However, generally, angels do not linger during such moments, as the negative energy transferred during sexual activity enters the woman's energy fields, especially if unconventional practices are involved, which angels do not favour.

283. Throughout pregnancy, does the child's angel stay with the mother?

During the entire course of pregnancy, the expectant mother is metaphorically cradled by Gabriel. This explains occasional and peculiar changes in food preferences and behaviour. Pregnancy can be considered a healing process, as the mother's bodily structures are practically being reconstructed throughout the gestation period, with Gabriel's influence prevalent.

284. How does one connect with angels?

Thought serves as the conduit. If one thinks with the intention of connecting with Michael, a connection with Michael is established. In Orthodoxy, the simplest form of connecting with angels is through the recitation of acathist hymns dedicated to them. As a prayer, the Annunciation prayer holds significance. Uttering a divinely inspired prayer automatically establishes a connection with the entity that inspired it—in the case of the Annunciation, the angel Gabriel.

285. Does the act of crossing oneself connect to angels?

Indeed, it does. However, not the Christic cross, but the one that emerges in the Old Testament as the symbol of Archangel Michael—preventing evil from transcending a certain threshold. The cross becomes a symbol that, once employed, aids in unlocking the gate to light, aligning individuals with the angels. It's crucial to note that the Christic cross isn't the sole positive symbol; each archangel boasts their own distinctive symbols. Utilising the Christic cross connects one with angels at the level of the Christic Heaven.

286. How do we discern which angels to invoke based on our desires?

For any gift, the prayer turns to Archangel Gabriel—the angel of bestowing gifts. While there are numerous specialised angels, summoning Gabriel suffices for any desired outcome: be it for children, financial gain, securing a job, or any other request. However, a deeper understanding of angels and their specialisations becomes essential. By seeking guidance from God—requesting the optimal angel for a specific desire, such as saying, "Lord, send me an angel to assist me with..."—we simplify the process.

287. Can we find ourselves without our angels, without guides?

Certainly. There exist various reasons why individuals might find themselves alone. One such instance is if one is forsaken by God due to their transgressions. Dr. George Ionescu, a psychiatry professor, posited that the role of a psychiatric doctor is akin to guiding the patient until they are once again embraced under God's protective wing.

Individuals can be left without angels, without guides, as a test of their faith. Every person undergoes a trial wherein God allows them to navigate life independently.

An additional circumstance where one might be without angels/guides is if they are taken through magical means or bound.

288. How can we reconnect with the source of light if we no longer have angels with us?

In instances of solitude, prayer emerges as the simplest means of connecting with the source of light. The source of light isn't distant but rather exists in the timeless. The key is to open the dimensions to the timeless, achieved through symbols like the cross, Reiki symbols, or visualisation. A recommended prayer is directed to the Mother, the Door of Mercy ("Open to us the door of mercy, O blessed Mother of God, Virgin, that we who hope in you may not perish but be saved through you from our needs, for you are the salvation of the Christian people"). This prayer uniquely opens gates from any location, particularly post-mortal existence when dimensions need opening.

289. How can we know that we've grown and received more angels of light?

Comparisons can be made with individuals from one's past, relics of saints, and holy places. The litmus test lies in how one perceives the energy in these comparisons, comparing current sensations with those from the past.

290. How can we know if we've grown in relation to angels?

Every sacred place harbours entities of light—angels. To ascertain personal growth, one might visit a holy place, perhaps a pilgrimage site, and gauge their feelings compared to previous visits. If a sense of peace and harmony prevails, and all personal structures resonate positively, it indicates growth. This explains why, at the initial stages of spiritual evolution, individuals may keenly feel the vibration of certain places. As they progress, the intensity diminishes, but an awareness of how the place wholly accepts them remains.

291. Can our angels be bound?

Certain individuals engage in binding and stealing angels due to the coveted associations of angels with light, wealth, power, beauty, and wisdom. Those lacking these divine attributes may attempt to bind angels for their own use.

292. What can we do to liberate our angels upon realisation that they've been bound?

While it isn't excessively complicated, angels may, at times, free themselves. Various techniques exist, but the primary strategy is to continually bestow them with light and power. This involves practices such as prayers, fasting, candle lighting, listening to high-vibration music, sending light to them—essentially, anything that aligns with high vibrations. These practices provide angels with the necessary light, enabling them to self-liberate.

293. Do angels possess IQ (intelligence quotient) and finite knowledge?

Angels share the same characteristics as humans and, as such, boast an IQ. While IQ is inherently finite, it can be heightened and upgraded. The completion of personal missions, whether as a guardian angel or within special assignments, allows angels to receive divine gifts and graces, such as wisdom, thereby elevating their IQ. Knowledge isn't a finite entity; akin to humans, it can be expanded through diverse activities, study, and general wisdom.

294. How can angels augment their capacity for free will?

The amplification of this capacity among angels is achievable through increased power, heightened vibration, and the acquisition of wisdom. Fulfilling personal missions results in the receipt of divine gifts and graces, effectively increasing their capacity for choice through inherent wisdom. Elevated vibration facilitates access to high-vibration thoughts, subsequently expanding the array of available choices.

295. Who is Metatron?

Archangel Metatron stands among the celestial titans, crafted before the dawn of the material Universe. Revered as one of the wisest and mightiest beings, he assumes the mantle of guardian over celestial enigmas, positioned as a mediator bridging the divine realms and humanity.

296. How may we commune with Metatron?

Given his profound wisdom, forging a connection with Metatron necessitates our spiritual traverse through a sequence of evolutionary phases. Initially, collaboration with our guardian angel beckons, progressing in tandem. Subsequently, engagement with archangels, seraphim, cherubim ensues, paving the way for an ascent to the echelon permitting access to Metatron.

297. Are there rites to access the energies of Metatron?

A more accessible avenue to tap into the energies of Metatron lies in the initiations within the Shamballa system or the Ascension Metatron system, wherein initiation entails interaction with four of Metatron's sacred symbols.

298. What armaments do warrior angels wield?

Diverging from the conventional image of Archangel Michael brandishing the sword of light, warrior angels boast an arsenal that transcends the realms of human imagination. In exigencies, the Almighty can dispatch warrior angels to enact cataclysmic fates upon a celestial body.

299. What characterises incarnated angels?

Much akin to the varied spectrum of spirits incarnating on Earth—offspring of the Divine, embodiments of feminine or masculine principles, extraterrestrial entities—angels too descend for an earthly sojourn, seeking to partake in the multifaceted tapestry of corporeal existence.

300. Why do angelic spirits choose earthly incarnation?

Primarily, the impetus for angels descending upon Earth lies in a profound transformation of their perceptions concerning the intricacies of worldly existence. Guardian angels, particularly, driven by an extensive history of collaborative missions with humanity, yearn to unravel the mysteries of embodied life.

301. What constitutes the principal objective of angels descending to Earth?

The celestial sojourn of angels onto Earth encompasses a comprehensive overhaul of their perceptual paradigm regarding the terrestrial sphere and the essence of life itself. Their earthly descent, a sagacious endeavour, positions them to explore the nuances of life within corporeal vessels.

302. How can one discern if they embody the spirit of an incarnated angel?

Discerning one's angelic incarnation unfolds through nuanced measurements, an innate sense of belonging in vibrantly elevated spaces, a palpable sense of distinction from others, and a detachment from conventional gender identifications—an inherent and distinct uniqueness.

303. Do incarnated angels retain memories of their celestial origins?

In the process of earthly embodiment, angels undergo a selective amnesia, a fundamental tenet designed for terrestrial existence. This lack of conscious awareness of their divine origins facilitates an unconscious manifestation of both benevolence and malevolence.

304. Do incarnated angels bear the obligatory mission of salvation for the lineage into which they are born, and the expiation of familial karma?

Not all incarnated angels are bound by such a mandate. While it remains an aspirational trajectory for optimal personal evolution to attend to the karmic fabric of the lineage into which one is born, certain angels choose earthly manifestation with explicit, mission-oriented objectives, divergent from familial karmic obligations. Those angels faithfully executing their designated missions inadvertently contribute to their personal advancement and that of their kin.

305. Do incarnated angels bear karma?

Incarnated angels typically undergo a sole incarnation. Instances of multiple incarnations are rare, arising when they fail to assimilate their lessons and fulfil personal missions. This is owing to their specific, punctual, and lucid missions. However, they do carry karma as any lack of comprehension as guardian angels regarding human choices, errors, judgments, or misguidance becomes their karma. Subsequently, upon incarnation, they "arrive" in the family or lineage they resonate with based on their karma.

Thus, despite potential discontent among them, questioning why they must shoulder the karma of a lineage when they lack human errors, it is simply because they resonated with that lineage and it is imperative to settle the debt. Fundamentally, everything they find awry in their lineage is the darkness that, through resonance, drew them to Earth.

306. What memories can incarnated angels access without other lives?

Conceivably, if an incarnated angel undergoes regression, they may perceive more lives, fragments from the lives of individuals they guarded as angels. They experience a life as an angel at various stages: as a child, adolescent, adult, and elderly. From the sum of these lives, the angel comprehends the true events on the earthly plane. As an incarnated spirit, they carry these life segments in their subconscious, accessible through regressions, shamanic journeys, etc. Nevertheless, in reality, they never lived these lives physically.

307. How does karma impact the spiritual awakening of an incarnated angel?

An incarnated angel can manifest free will based on their karma, akin to any other incarnated spirit. The greater the karma, the smaller the capacity to manifest free will. In this sense, personal karma influences them through negative programs at an internal level, which manifest externally.

308. If an incarnated angel has light karma, is their spiritual awakening less affected?

Should an incarnated angel not bear heavy karma, a common scenario since God promptly sends them to incarnation if they misbehave, and they don't accumulate much karma, they may have less light karma from their lineage. For instance, an angel who made mistakes in guiding a human, accumulating personal karma, is sent to Earth to understand and learn. However, if, in the meantime, they judged, became upset with humans, etc., they are drawn to a lineage where these flaws will manifest. Why? To help humans understand and learn. In this case, they might land in a family where the lineage's karma is not light.

309. How does the maternal lineage's karma affect the spiritual awakening of incarnated angels?

Incarnated angels automatically inherit issues from their maternal lineage—parents, ancestors, etc. Spiritual awakening leads to the capacity to manifest free will but is hindered by maternal karma that emotionally blocks them. This is particularly evident in the inability to exercise free will in relationships, not just romantic but all kinds.

310. How does the paternal lineage's karma affect the spiritual awakening of incarnated angels?

The spiritual awakening of an incarnated angel is obstructed by paternal karma, not only in material aspects but also in other facets. The paternal lineage's karma, encompassing aspects like material success, tenacity, finances, profession, achievement in sports, hampers the manifestation of free will and materialises divine will.

311. How does a partner's karma influence the spiritual awakening of incarnated angels?

Incarnated angels are generally attractive as partners due to their light and the intuitive sense that life improves unconsciously with an incarnated angel. However, if a partner has heavy karma, it affects the spiritual awakening of the incarnated angel. Through their harmonisation, the issues of the partner will automatically impede the angel.

312. How does the birth of an incarnated angel influence the lives of parents?

It depends on the divine characteristics and rights of the incarnated angel. For instance, if an angel made significant mistakes as a guardian angel, having profound lessons in incarnation, it negatively influences the divine right to wealth in the family into which they are born. However, if the angel comes with significant divine potential and rights, the family's divine rights increase automatically, enhancing all positive aspects of the family.

313. Is there a blockage preventing incarnated angels from measuring accurately?

Yes, incarnated angels often fear discovering truths about themselves or others. Incarnated angels intuitively follow 91% to 94% of God's will, but the remainder follows their will. To have an excuse for not knowing God's will, many prefer not to measure.

314. Why do incarnated angels believe they are always right?

It stems from the pride of angels in God's service. While it's true that in many cases, incarnated angels are right, when left without divine wisdom, they believe they know everything, leading to mistakes

315. Do incarnated angels encounter difficulty in acknowledging their mistakes?

Indeed, they grapple with this challenge precisely because they harbour the impression that fallibility eludes them, making it arduous to confess errors and utter the humbling phrase "forgive me," a poignant demonstration of humility.

316. What are the paramount predicaments of fallen angels?

They include a pervasive fear of erring in the eyes of God, an inability to forgive oneself, a profound sense of guilt and wrongdoing before the Divine, a deficiency in self-esteem, and an overarching pride—all deeply rooted in the Luciferic descent.

317. For what reason do incarnated angels seek recognition?

Their distinctiveness and perceived superiority propel them to desire acknowledgment naturally. From a certain vantage point, they consider themselves superior to their human counterparts and find it only fitting to receive due recognition.

318. Can an angel harbour false beliefs?

Indeed, an angel might adhere to beliefs such as the exclusive divinity of their God until an encounter with another God from a disparate realm alters their perspective.

319. How does the shadow of incarnated angels manifest?

The shadow of incarnated angels materialises through the individuals closely connected to them—partners, parents, children, friends, superiors, subordinates, and the like. In essence, the imperfections of incarnated angels mirror those of their parental figures.

320. Can an incarnated angel bear fears stemming from past guidance mistakes that manifest in their present life?

Certainly. If, in a previous existence, an angel misguided an individual to the point of their demise, they may carry the fear of drowning, flying, driving, and the like into their current incarnation.

321. Does an incarnated angel possess a shadow?

Undeniably. Each incarnated angel possesses a shadow—a realm of darkness and dense energy. Within this shadow lie unresolved aspects, misunderstood elements, negative emotions, hindrances, fears, phobias, false beliefs, superstitions, and more.

322. From where do incarnated angels derive false beliefs, superstitions, fears, and erroneous thought patterns?

Incarnated angels may inherit superstitions, false beliefs, fears, and phobias from those they once guided as guardian angels. Their resistance to correction is heightened due to a perception of omniscience, making it arduous to relinquish these ingrained patterns.

323. Can incarnated angels inherit the emotional traumas of those they once guarded as guardian angels?

Yes, they can. When an individual experiences emotional wounds, perceived injustices, abandonment, rejection, or betrayal, both the guardian angel and God resonate with these sentiments. Thus, incarnated angels may carry the emotional traumas of the humans they once safeguarded.

324. Does an incarnated angel with a higher astral age find it more challenging or easier to love oneself?

There is no direct correlation between astral age and an incarnated angel's ability to love oneself. It solely depends on one's perception of oneself.

325. Does an angel with a higher astral age heal from traumas more easily, or is it contingent on individual efforts?

The healing of traumas and personal evolution is a product of one's personal efforts and is unrelated to astral age. At times, a higher astral age might even hinder the process, as individuals may perceive themselves as self-sufficient and not in need of healing.

326. What is the love language specific to incarnated angels?

Words. They possess a distinct need for recognition, verbal expressions of love, and appreciation for who they are.

327. How is the love of an incarnated angel experienced?

When an incarnated angel falls in love, this sentiment can originate from various sources. If they feel the emotion of love localised in the heart, it is not their own love. Love from the soul is essentially God's love for that person. In other words, when I meet someone and find them pleasant, on a soul level, I am aware that it's not my love but rather God's love at the level I've reached for that person, for reasons known only to Him.

328. How can incarnated angels differentiate between self-love they feel towards someone and God's love for that person?

The love that persists when the soul steps aside is self-love. Because of this confusion, many people experience contradictory emotions—alternating between self-love and self-hatred. When measured at the level of self, they might not love themselves at all, potentially even harbouring murderous intentions. The reason is that God loves both individuals, so the incarnated angel feels God's love for the partner. However, when the soul steps aside, for instance during sexual encounters, and they remain at the self level, they may be enemies from past lives, causing mutual suffering in this life.

329. For what reasons might incarnated angels be upset with the Sons of God from past lives?

There are instances of angels who are displeased with the Sons of God for not heeding their guidance in past lives.

Significant grievances arise, and when they encounter each other in this life, conflicts may arise. Conversely, Sons of God might resent their angelic guardians for what they perceive as abandonment during challenging times. However, they fail to realise that, at that moment, the angel was carrying out the will of God, and their guardianship had reached its conclusion.

330. How can incarnated angels concretely determine the source of their self-directed resentment towards someone?

Firstly, it's crucial to recognise that the love they feel is not from the self and that, in reality, they don't love that person. This resentment may stem from this life or a past one. Nevertheless, such resentment arises from ignorance. One can explore the spiritual realm, for instance, through regression, to understand the origin of the resentment between a spirit and another, an angel and a son of God, or vice versa.

331. Can incarnated angels live in dark spaces?

Angels of light, when incarnated, disdain darkness and cannot thrive in small, dark spaces. Those of darker inclinations, however, find comfort in both light and darkness.

332. How can incarnated angels contribute to the awakening of those in the family they are born into?

While they cannot directly facilitate spiritual awakening—reserved for God's timing—they can contribute to their family's evolution and karmic payments. Their mere presence can transmute negative energies and past programming. Additionally, they often serve as a spiritual role model.

333. Can incarnated angels carry the karma of their partner after marriage?

It depends on the partner's karma and the astral age of the incarnated angel. If the angel has a higher astral age than the partner, they might not feel the impact. Conversely, if their astral age is lower than the partner's, the partner's karma might overwhelm them.

334. From which echelon do incarnated angels descend to absolve ancestral karma?

The payment of ancestral karma is not contingent on the origin level of the incarnated angel but on the intention and realisation of the ancestral karma payment.

335. What does it signify when an incarnated angel attains enlightenment?

It signifies that the respective spirit has reached a stratum where it possesses and radiates its own light—a celestial luminary without hierarchical bounds.

336. How can incarnated angels attain enlightenment?

The paramount element of enlightenment is spiritual gold. In essence, if one possesses gold, one possesses light; lacking gold results in a deficit of illumination.

337. What is the spectrum of astral age values for incarnated angels?

Incarnated angels can span ages slightly surpassing that of Earth (over 4 billion years). As per my encounters, some may exceed 18 billion years, within the context of our Universe, which is 15.4 billion years old.

338. Why are an increasing number of incarnated angels descending to Earth?

Primarily, it is to counterbalance the transgressions committed by humans. Additionally, it serves to elevate the planet's vibrational frequency, impart spiritual and technological insights, and implement divine strategies on the terrestrial plane.

339. Are the 144,000 chosen by God incarnated angels?

No. They emanate from fallen angels, transmute into Sons of God through incarnation, and subsequently relapse, reverting to mere mortals.

340. What societal role do incarnated angels generally assume?

On Earth, through the medium of incarnated angels, God forges social hierarchies—educational systems, military structures, political factions, and more.

341. Are incarnated angels conducive to business?

Certainly. The majority of incarnated angels may harbour personal missions to generate wealth.

342. Does the employment of incarnated angels in firms or companies augment the divine entitlement to wealth and success for the entity?

In numerous instances, incarnated angels possess divine entitlements to substantial wealth. Their magnitude, as well as their celestial origin, correlates with the magnitude of their divine entitlements, thereby automatically enhancing the divine entitlement to wealth and success for the entity or workplace they integrate. There exist firms dedicated to personnel recruitment collaborating with paranormals or individuals possessing expertise in this domain, actively seeking incarnated angels to integrate into various firms, companies, and institutions

343. An angel incarnate, upon completing their earthly mission, will they proceed to incarnate on another celestial body?

If they bear a personal mission there, indeed. However, it is not obligatory, as the Earthly experience might prove sufficient.

344. How does an incarnated angel discern their divine allegiance?

It proves rather elusive. One potential solution involves radiesthetic measurements or, during the Holy Liturgy, positioning oneself at the church's centre beneath the dome and, through visualisation, ascending to the level of their God (i.e., permitting their spirit to reach toward the light) and observing the relationship with the Christic God from that vantage. If their spirit surpasses Jesus, they belong to a God from a loftier Heaven.

345. Do incarnated angels possess the prerogative to enhance their mission?

Indeed, they are permitted to beseech God for the augmentation of their mission, adhering to the same conditions applicable to all incarnated spirits.

346. What is the yin-yang equilibrium among incarnated angels, and what traits do they embody?

The yin-yang equilibrium for incarnated angels is 50-50, contingent upon whom they serve, the Mother or God the Father, determining whether they predominantly exhibit masculine or feminine characteristics. Consequently, male incarnated angels might project a subtly effeminate aura, and female incarnated angels, notwithstanding their general beauty, may manifest unmistakable internal masculine traits.

347. Is there a preordained path for champions who are incarnated angels?

It is often asserted that champions aren't crafted but rather revealed. However, being a champion implies possessing potential or talent in a specific field, be it sports, art, or science. Yet, genuine champions are those who toil diligently. Frequently, hard work, training, and physical, intellectual, or spiritual effort prove more pivotal than innate talent. An incarnated angel may indeed be preprogrammed to become a champion. However, on Earth, temptations, obstacles, and trials can impede the angel from realising their plan to be a champion. In other words, an angel, too, can lose their way.

348. In which vocations are most incarnated angels found?

Depending on what they need to learn, incarnated angels can be found in any profession, even those considered less esteemed.

349. Why are incarnated angels found in professions like hairstylists or barbers?

Engaging with people, tending to their heads and hair, by the mere act of placing their hands on people's heads and hair, effectively cleanses them of negative energies. They absorb those negative energies and transmute them. Alongside masseurs, therapists, and sex workers, they serve as a kind of spiritual sanitation workers.

350. Why are many incarnated angels in the medical field?

Incarnated angels who become doctors are usually former archangels who have taken human lives and have a mission to learn to love and assist humans.

351. Why are many incarnated angels in IT, robotics, and cybernetic engineering?

They are sent by God to develop technology, laying the

foundations for a material future based on computers and robots.

352. What role do incarnated angels play in aviation?

In aviation, you often find spirits with advanced astral ages, whether incarnated angels or children of God, both as pilots and flight attendants. Their role is to ensure the protection of flights because large angels can withstand the negative spirits present in storms, turbulence, and the like.

353. Are there incarnated angels in positions of power?

Indeed, there are incarnated angels who create hierarchical social systems, ministries, schools, universities, armies, and political hierarchies, with special missions for Earth.

354. Are there incarnated angels in contact sports?

Yes, there are angels who come to learn to fight, to battle for Heaven, and in their incarnation, they may participate in sports such as martial arts.

355. Is there fate or destiny given the free will of an incarnated angel?

The free will of an incarnated angel is akin to the free will we have in a school where we have required and optional subjects. Some things are imposed, and the manifestation of free will is how you navigate through the predetermined and mandated subject matter (fate). There are optional subjects where you can express your free will, but we all have required subjects through which we learn on this planet, including incarnated angels.

356. Is the existence of incarnated angels predetermined on Earth?

Incarnation, life on Earth, is effectively imposed upon fallen angels by God to instill an understanding of good and evil. Thus, each of us on this planet is here as a consequence of this imposition. Despite life being thrust upon us, we retain the freedom to choose how we navigate it. Even for incarnated angels, who generally arrive with unique personal missions, there exists free will in determining how they fulfil their purpose.

357. What is the overarching personal mission of incarnated angels?

Their mission encompasses aiding and redeeming their ancestors, settling the karmic debts of their lineage, gaining wisdom, comprehending the spiritual principles governing Earthly life, advancing in spiritual power, and generating soul/spiritual gold for the God from which they originate.

358. What specific tasks might incarnated angels undertake?

These celestial beings can embark on a plethora of missions. Examples include venturing into space, assuming roles as leading scientists introducing groundbreaking technologies, inventions, and discoveries; becoming influential leaders who leave an indelible mark on history; or evolving into saintly figures.

359. Can an incarnated angel be ensnared?

Indeed, an incarnated angel may find themselves bound by someone wielding knowledge and mastery in the astral realm, akin to the predicament of Gulliver in the land of Lilliput. This could involve the extraction of their soul, theft of divine potentials, constriction of energy fields, blockage of energy centres, and interference with their connection to God. Importantly, all of these interventions occur with the consent of God, serving as a form of spiritual education and karmic settlement.

360. Why are incarnated angels drawn to demons?

The attraction of incarnated angels to demons lies in the harmonising dynamic between them. Even though some light is forfeited in the process, incarnated angels absorb the darkness of the demon, transmuting it into light and converting it into spiritual gold. Moreover, a key mission of incarnated angels is to facilitate the return of fallen angels, or demons, to God.

361. Is the physical body of incarnated angels akin to that of humans?

No, the physical form of incarnated angels is composed of divine structures resembling layers of an onion. These structures, possessing exceedingly high vibrations, would wreak havoc on the physical body if not shielded. The higher an incarnated angel originates, the more activated divine structures are present in their corporeal form.

362. Do incarnated angels require darkness?

Yes, a balance between light and darkness is essential for the existence of the physical body. The more light an angel possesses, the greater the need for darkness to maintain equilibrium. The optimal ratio is 81% light to 19% darkness. Incarnated angels absorb this darkness through various activities such as sports, sex, relationships, consumption of certain foods (like meat), smoking, and exposure to certain music genres. This balance is contextualised for everyday life; however, engaging in activities like car racing or boxing may necessitate an increased percentage of darkness, subsequently restored to equilibrium.

363. Do incarnated angels have the right to observe black fasting, and can they?

Observing black fasting is not universally permissible for incarnated angels because it can dismantle lower physical structures and bring the individual closer to the level of the self. If the self operates at a very high vibration, an incarnated angel might experience severe discomfort while practicing black fasting. This form of fasting is primarily recommended for incarnated angels burdened with significant ancestral karma, as the resulting veil of darkness is sufficiently large to shield the physical body.

364. How does the ability of incarnated angels to give and receive love compare to that of humans?

Incarnated angels, in comparison to humans, encounter challenges in giving and receiving love across various relationships, be it with partners, children, parents, or humanity at large. Having previously existed within the love of God, they are accustomed to receiving love rather than reciprocating it. The absence of God's love on Earth creates a sense of nostalgia for the lost paradise, as they grapple with the lesson of learning to love during their incarnation. Many incarnated angels feel the essence of love within their souls but find themselves incapable of expressing it at the level of the self. Humans, in contrast, have had the opportunity to experience love from maternal instincts in animals to the love shared among people.

365. Are incarnated angels considered superior to humans?

From certain perspectives, incarnated angels exhibit superiority to humans in terms of potentials, qualities, inner light, and the ability to discern between good and evil, truth and falsehood. However, humans can demonstrate superiority through qualities such as love, compassion, camaraderie, and a spirit of teamwork. Humans possess attributes that incarnated angels are in the process of acquiring, and vice versa.

366. Do Archangels incarnated on Earth undergo a distinct evolution compared to other incarnated angels?

Incarnated Archangels typically served as guardians for priests, monks, and warriors engaged in lethal pursuits. Guiding these individuals led to a profound connection to the suffering inflicted on those who fell, as well as their families. Consequently, they bear the weight of lessons in suffering, often manifesting as unexplained panic attacks. Additionally, they grapple with lessons in love and sexuality, aspects they may not have fully comprehended in their roles as guardians of monks. Now unbound by vows of chastity, poverty, and obedience, they find themselves detached from these previous commitments. Their Earthly journey involves learning to love humanity, life, their own bodies (many of which previously disregarded the feminine), self-love, and love for all.

367. What are the consequences if an incarnated angel refuses (without divine consent) to exit a marriage?

Primarily, they lose a part of their soul for straying from their destined path, forfeiting divine protection. Subsequently, a series of challenges unfold, including accidents, financial losses, disputes, and illnesses, all stemming from the choice of solitude.

368. Who is closer to love and sexuality, humans, or angels?

Humans are closer. Angels, unaccustomed to experiencing love at the level of the self, come to Earth to learn the lesson of love. Humans, possessing denser energy (chi) and more darkness, find themselves more proximate to sexuality than angels' light.

369. Do incarnated angels emerge from higher celestial realms than Jesus and become Christian priests? Why?

Angels descending from above the Christic level are baptised at birth when their selves are dormant. This initiation aligns them with larger angels from the Christic Ninth Heaven. Some, inadvertently, find themselves becoming Christian priests. As they undergo spiritual awakening, a sense of dissonance may arise, leading many to abandon their priesthood. Christian institutions actively seek these higher angels to enhance the power of the church and, consequently, of Jesus.

370. What are the most challenging lessons for incarnated female angels?

Among the most arduous lessons are femininity, female sexuality, and motherhood. The majority of female angels were guardians of males, embodying psychic traits with masculine attributes. Motherhood poses challenges as they fear pregnancy, the pain of childbirth, and the responsibility of raising a child. Moreover, grappling with feminine sexuality, distinct from the masculine, remains an essential lesson.

371. What are the most challenging lessons for incarnated male angels?

The most challenging lesson is embracing masculinity. Incarnated angels exhibit a yin-yang balance of 50/50, resulting in men born with seemingly effeminate qualities. Consequently, they need to learn masculine characteristics such as willpower, tenacity, courage, the ability to lead, and male sexuality.

372. What is the greatest suffering for incarnated angels?

Their most significant suffering emanates from the yearning for the lost paradise. Feeling rejected by Heaven and God due to their assignment to Earth, they harbour resentment, manifesting as wounds of rejection and abandonment. Female angels may also contend with feelings of betrayal for incarnating as women.

373. Can an incarnated angel remain bound to Earth after death?

Yes, under certain circumstances. Major mistakes, the loss or sale of their soul, or emotional ties to another person through love, hatred, or unforgiveness may leave an angel bound to the Earthly plane.

374. What must an angel do to return home if they have erred and become bound to Earth, unable to ascend to heaven?

Primarily, they need to seek God's forgiveness. Subsequently, the desire to return to heaven must be genuine, as some angels may grow attached to Earthly life. Redemption of the soul, producing more spiritual gold than lost, becomes essential.

375. Are incarnated angels obliged to consume a specific type of food?

No, depending on their vibration, personal or ancestral karma, angels can eat anything, including meat, if it proves beneficial. Higher vibrational angels may consume a variety of foods, including meat, cola, and engage in habits like smoking, to balance their energies. Those with heavy karma may feel compelled to fast.

376. Why do incarnated angels have a lesson in sexuality?

Because they need to learn to manifest love in the physical realm. Considering sex a sin, they must learn to sublimate sexual energy into spiritual gold. They also need to learn to be parents, the lessons of pregnancy and childbirth (for angelic women).

377. Why are incarnated angels attracted to the underworld?

Incarnated angels are drawn to the underworld because they are attracted to the demons in that realm. Since incarnated angels do not have a high level of sexuality, they derive pleasure through their partner's pleasure. If the partner is astrally young, their sexual energy will be small, and the angel will not feel anything. However, if the partner has significant demons, the incarnated angel feels through those demons.

378. Why are incarnated angels attracted to rock music?

Because rock music opens portals to the underworld and emits negative energy. Incarnated angels need to absorb negative energy to live on Earth.

379. What can negatively affect the mental health of an incarnated angel?

Blocking the higher chakras due to ancestral karma from the opposite-sex parent. For instance, if oral sex is performed without energetic cleansing, it reduces brain vibration. Magic can also affect an incarnated angel's mental health if God allows them to manifest wisdom from the self or if God abandons them.

380. Under what conditions can an incarnated angel be abandoned by God, and what does that mean?

Even an incarnated angel can be abandoned by God

when they consistently ignore their guardian angel or God's voice. This means they no longer receive guidance, help, advice, or power from God. It doesn't mean they leave God, but God and the guardian angel no longer intervene.

381. Can an incarnated angel be possessed by a demon?

An incarnated angel can be possessed by a demon larger than them or if they have made a pact with the demon, or if they are unaware that a demon has interrupted their connection with their originating God.

382. How can an incarnated angel escape the negative influence of a demon?

Through prayer, burning candles, pilgrimages to holy places, black fasting (within limits), high-vibration music, and rituals or services in churches, mosques, temples, synagogues, etc.

383. Do incarnated angels believe that one must be deserving to attain their desires?

Statistically speaking, based on my observations, incarnated angels tend to hold the belief that they are entitled to everything they desire. However, they often find themselves dissatisfied due to a lack of recognition and assistance from those around them.

384. Do incarnated angels encounter difficulties in adapting to life on Earth?

Since they have not previously experienced life on this planet, they often struggle to understand the rules and spiritual principles that govern Earth. This lack of familiarity can lead to errors in judgment. Furthermore, they tend to perceive the world in black-and-white terms, struggling with the concept of ambiguity.

385. Is there a hierarchical structure among incarnated angels on Earth, similar to the celestial hierarchy of angels?

No, there isn't. Each spirit that undergoes incarnation on Earth embarks on its journey from an equal starting point. The hierarchies that existed prior to their birth no longer apply. It's akin to a scenario where a general and a soldier run a race together, side by side. However, distinctions are still made based on factors such as astral age, inner strength, intelligence, and the power of the soul. Despite these differences, all incarnated angels are considered equals on Earth. Instinctively, individuals who were once subordinates often acknowledge and involuntarily defer to those with greater experience.

386. How do incarnated angels evolve through Reiki initiations?

Through the process of initiation and the receipt of the Dragon's breath from their master, incarnated angels gain access to new potentials, experience an increase in inner strength and dimension, and absorb information, energy, light, and soul from their master during the initiation. They also receive the assistance of angels and spirits participating in the initiation. Additionally, they gain access to the light channeling through the Holy Spirit at the Reiki level.

387. Can an incarnated angel bestow light upon a saint?

Indeed, they can. Christian saints represent spirits who, through their evolutionary journey on Earth and beyond, have reached the exalted realms of the 8th, 9th, or 10th heaven within the Christic Heaven. However, there exist incarnated angels who hail from spiritual levels higher than the Christic realms. Consequently, they possess access to energies surpassing those available to Christian saints. As a result, they have the capability to bestow light upon these saints. This dynamic extends to saints from any religious or belief system.

388. What is the relationship between incarnated female angels and motherhood?

Incarnated angels lack firsthand experience in motherhood, which leads to an unconscious fear of maternity, childbirth, and the responsibilities of child-rearing. This often results in them suppressing their desire to conceive, even for angelic fathers who are themselves incarnated angels, despite their mental desire for children.

389. What are incarnated angels' perspectives on their own birth?

A significant majority of incarnated angels make a single journey into incarnation, and as such, they do not possess the experience of their own birth. In the realm of angels, the act of birth is synonymous with a fall from grace, signifying the loss of divine potentials and the transformation into a lesser state. Consequently, such an experience is often regarded as traumatic.

390. How do incarnated angels approach the institution of marriage?

Incarnated angels generally harbour an aversion to marriage and the prospect of being tied down. However, marriage is frequently viewed as a vital life lesson—a school of sorts—enabling them to gain a deeper understanding of commitment and family life.

391. What is the stance of incarnated angels regarding divorce?

In most cases, incarnated angels adhere to divine will, choosing to marry and divorce in accordance with God's plan. They may remain in a marriage even if they no longer desire it, viewing it as a personal mission.

392. Do incarnated angels engage in deceit within romantic relationships?

Incarnated angels may, on occasion, resort to deception, yet their motivations for such actions carry unique connotations. Primarily, incarnated angels residing beyond the realm of the Christic consciousness do not bind themselves to the precepts of Christian doctrine, and hence, they may not strictly adhere to those principles. Deception, when it occurs, often unfolds as a result of their simultaneous personal duties and missions to multiple partners. It can function as a lesson to their romantic companions, serving to teach virtues like forgiveness, the liberation from jealousy, and relinquishment of possessiveness.

This behaviour can be attributed to the lessons these angels need to learn. For instance, they may have strongly condemned adultery during previous lifetimes when they functioned as incarnated angels, only to undergo such experiences firsthand to gain profound insights. They are compelled to traverse the spectrum of actions they once censured in the human beings they guided - be it adultery, abortion, or deceit.

393. Do incarnated angels harbour a fear of death?

Incarnated angels do indeed experience a fear of death, stemming from the realisation that they shall stand before the divine presence, their apprehensions centring around unfulfilled personal missions.

394. Can incarnated angels petition for a modification or augmentation of their designated missions?

Much like any other incarnated spirit, incarnated angels hold the prerogative to seek changes, enhancements, or diversifications within their personal missions. This endeavour necessitates an initial exploration to determine the nature of their missions. For instance, they may have been assigned roles as psychoanalysts and subsequently grow weary of these duties. Upholding their free will, they can choose to conclude their psychoanalyst mission under the condition of training six new psychoanalysts to take their place, thus ensuring the absence of a void. This process enables them to request or select, in harmony with the divine will, entirely new personal missions aligned with their inherent attributes, talents, and aptitudes.

395. What characterises incarnated dark angels?

The chief characteristic of incarnated dark angels lies in their remarkable capacity to discern the dichotomies between good and evil, truth and falsehood. As denizens of the astral realm, these angels face relentless trials from demons, who strive to deceive them into passing through the celestial gates. They possess an extraordinary intuition for immediately detecting lies, pretence, evil forces, and demonic influences. However, it is imperative to underscore that despite these challenges, dark incarnated angels remain benevolent themselves.

386. How do incarnated angels distinguish themselves from other incarnated spirits?

Incarnated angels are notably characterised by their unwavering obstinacy. From a tender age, they tend to grapple with any form of authority, especially those emanating from figures they perceive as spiritually inferior. This is primarily owing to their profound inner understanding of their missions, thereby instinctively repelling individuals whom they deem lacking in spiritual stature.

397. What behavioural traits typify incarnated angels?

Incorporated angels frequently exhibit a resolute and indomitable demeanour, particularly evident in those descending from higher echelons, such as the archangels. They commonly manifest resistance towards any form of authority, whether emanating from parents, superiors, or spouses, underpinned by their intrinsic cognisance of their life's purpose. Consequently, they often find themselves grappling with the intricacies of relationships involving individuals they discern as less spiritually advanced. However, it is imperative to recognise that incarnated angels from higher echelons exhibit distinct behavioural attributes. Their demeanour does not encompass resistance to authority; their true nature radiates luminously.

398. What are the temptations that beset incarnated angels?

Incarnated angels are more frequently susceptible to temptations within the material realm in comparison to other incarnated spirits. This vulnerability primarily arises due to their dearth of prior experience in this plane. Furthermore, their sense of pride during their incarnated state tends to escalate alongside their ego, rendering them prone to committing various imprudent actions.

399. Do incarnated angels perceive themselves as exceptional compared to others?

In their initial stages of incarnation, incarnated angels often foster misguided beliefs, viewing themselves as unique entities, which, in some instances, leads to consequential errors. However, divine intervention follows their indiscretions, instigating self-awareness. Consequently, they come to the profound realisation that they are no superior to incarnated demons and dragons. Furthermore, while incarnated angels may not consciously recognise it, they occasionally develop deep affection for incarnated demons, serpents, and dragons, who may serve as their parents, siblings, lovers, or children. Within the divine wisdom, God has devised a means of reconciliation in such relationships.

400. By the principle of resonance, is it necessary for incarnated angels to incarnate through at least one parent who is an angel or a Child of God?

Incarnated angels may indeed be born through individuals of any background, provided there exists no substantial disparity in astral age in comparison to one of the parents.

401. What types of spirits can give birth to incarnated angels?

Incarnated angels can be born through parents of any spiritual background. While it holds true that parents should possess certain attributes to facilitate a particular form of upbringing and life for their children, it is equally imperative that a vibrational and astral age connection exists between the parent and the incarnated angelic child.

402. What level of vibrational resonance must parents possess to give birth to an incarnated angel?

In general, incarnated angels resonate with at least one of their two parents, sharing an inner light akin to that parent. The difference in vibrational frequency typically amounts to only one or two celestial tiers between the parent and the incarnated angel. Their astral ages should not differ significantly, as this misalignment would prove toxic.

403. Can guardian angels fall in love with those they protect or other individuals?

Angels can indeed experience love for humans, a parallel to the Sons of God's affection for Earthly women, culminating in the birth of demigods and giants as recounted in Genesis. However, angels must embody themselves to consummate this love, an act regarded as a fall from grace. This embodiment serves as a means for them to explore the lessons of carnal, terrestrial love.

404. Can incarnated angels become entangled in the earthly plane through successive incarnations?

Should they fail to grasp the lessons they've incarnated to learn, incarnated angels, like other spirit entities, will repeatedly return until they do. Their primary lesson often revolves around love, but it is not an exclusive focus. Any misguided counsel they have provided or misunderstandings they have harboured while guiding humans become pivotal lessons during their incarnations. Each angel is bound to seek the demons they are meant to nurture and help guide back to God. Until that mission is accomplished, they remain entangled in the earthly realm, ensnared in the illusions of this world. They come to the realisation that without God, there is no prospect of returning, and they gain insight into the immense challenges of being human. They comprehend the countless eons required to traverse the physical body's trials before the path home to the heavens is cleared.

405. What is the mission of angels incarnating on Earth?

Incarnated angels undertake a variety of missions during their earthly sojourns, in addition to the fundamental lessons they must internalise. Their missions may encompass areas like education, conception, construction, or warfare. Upon their return to the celestial realm, they are, at the very least, positioned at the heaven level from which they originated, contingent on how proficiently they execute their tasks during their incarnations. Depending on their progression through these embodied experiences, they can ascend to the status of planetary archistrategists, becoming deities governing entire planets, or even entire universes.

406. How do the physical relationships between two incarnated angels materialise?

Relationships between two incarnated angels often prove unexciting, as their similar vibrations leave them bereft of the potential for mutual attraction. Consequently, such relationships are relatively rare or short-lived. They may convene for specific purposes, such as conceiving a child or uniting to confront significant demons.

407. How do the physical relationships between an incarnated angel and an incarnated Son of God unfold?

Such relationships are typically the most common. Incarnated Sons of God often encounter an incarnated angel who previously served as their guardian angel in prior incarnations. This rekindles a profound connection and trust, further kindled by the vibrational disparity between the two, generating sexual attraction.

408. How do the physical relationships between an incarnated angel and a masculine or feminine principle transpire?

When the incarnated principle originates from a similar celestial level as the angel or an even higher realm, the angel might find themselves in a subordinate role or vice versa. The dynamics are contingent upon the specific lessons the principle is meant to acquire during that incarnation, such as lessons in obedience.

409. How does anger manifest in incarnated angels?

Differing from most other incarnated spirits, incarnated angels grapple with forgiveness. They must learn the essential lesson of forgiveness, yet they initially harbour a strong determination to inflict harm, obstruct, manipulate, or inadvertently penalise individuals they may be angry with.

410. How do incarnated angels experience their connection with God and the heavenly realm from which they originate in the physical plane?

The physical body of an incarnated angel comprises structures drawn from the heavenly realm of their origin, extending down to Earth. As a consequence, their corporeal form inherently comprehends its purpose far more astutely than their conscious mind. By attending to the signals their body conveys, they can decipher God's expectations and gain insights into matters like dietary choices, travel destinations, film preferences, and the selection of partners. When an incarnated angel unites their consciousness, soul, and self, they establish a profound connection with the God from whom they originated.

411. What are the signs through which an incarnated angel can discern that they are no longer receiving information from the God of the heavenly realm from which they originate?

First and foremost, signs of unease become evident. An incapacity to harmonise their physical vessel arises. Unexplained headaches, akin to the sensation of a collapsing ceiling, manifest. Paradoxical emotional fluctuations become apparent, coupled with a palpable absence of the joy of existence, empathy, and love from the core. A tempest of negative thoughts prevails, culminating in nightmares, and more.

412. Is it possible for angels to attain a state of superconsciousness during an incarnation?

Any spirit has the potential to reach a state of superconsciousness, although not every incarnation necessitates its attainment. Some may have missions focused on healing or be solely geared towards lessons in love and family. To draw a parallel, if superconsciousness represents a subject at a doctoral level in mathematics, an individual might merely be required to pass an eighth-grade examination in this lifetime. Nevertheless, it is indeed true that there are spirits that astound even the Divine with their exceedingly swift spiritual evolution within the span of a single lifetime.

413. Can angels born on Earth possess astral ages older than our universe?

Especially in the era we currently traverse, spirits hailing from universes significantly older than ours incarnate on Earth. Incarnated angels with astral ages far surpassing 15 billion years do exist. These angels display characteristics distinct from the norm on our rather sexually-oriented planet. Their sexual desires are less pronounced, and they exhibit a greater emotional and mental equilibrium.

414. Why do angels from other universes incarnate on Earth?

Angels from other universes take on diverse purposes when incarnating on Earth. Their journey into this world is meant to teach them how to be human, for living as a human is no small feat. It entails navigating relationships, confronting loss, addressing issues of sexuality, and grappling with the various challenges of our world. These angels bring novel insights and serve as catalysts for the social and spiritual evolution of our planet. Many of them become educators, revolutionaries, or pioneers in various domains, sparking revolutions of a spiritual, industrial, and scientific nature to elevate the planet spiritually.

415. What is the connection between incarnated angels and spiritual gold?

Every incarnated angel is dispatched to Earth with the purpose of generating spiritual gold. They function as solar batteries that require constant recharging with spiritual gold which they then transmit back to the God from whom they originated.

416. In a sporting competition, are incarnated angels favoured over other incarnated spirits?

No, in a competitive context, the determinants are diligence and effort.

417. If an incarnated angel lacks inherent talents or athletic abilities, can they acquire them?

Indeed, through persistent effort or the 'art of obtaining grace,' one can acquire any aptitude or talent they lack.

418. Do incarnated angels have a penchant for dance?

Not all incarnated angels possess an inherent affinity for dance. For instance, battle archangels are not naturally predisposed to dancing. Nevertheless, angels from higher celestial realms are indeed engaged in dance. Through their dance, they open gateways to higher realms of consciousness, exemplified in the dervish whirling dance where dancers move around the point where the self, the soul, and consciousness intersect, thus unlocking the path to superconsciousness.

419. Which of the dances performed by incarnated angels is the one closest to divinity?

The dance of the whirling dervishes, followed by ballet, and subsequently, the others.

420. What role do incarnated angels play in the realms of research and education?

Within the spheres of knowledge and education, incarnated angels are tasked with fostering the development of their respective fields, propelling their evolution, and unearthing novel discoveries. They serve as the vanguards of innovation, instruments through which God herself facilitates the societal progress.

421. What does an incarnated angel bestow upon their life partner?

In essence, incarnated angels possess a corporeal form predominantly composed of divine structures. Engaging in a relationship with an incarnated angel, through harmonisation, be it through the sharing of meals, physical intimacy, or even the act of sleeping together, provides the partner with access to the entirety of the angel's divine structures. This access allows the partner to reach a level as permitted by the God of the respective angel.

422. What does it signify when an incarnated angel carries out the will of God but refrains from direct involvement in its realisation?

In certain scenarios, an incarnated angel may set their corporeal form, composed of divine structures and sub-personalities, into an autonomous state for all activities, be it their occupation, sexual relations, culinary endeavours, and more. Meanwhile, their core self remains detached, uninvolved in these activities.

423. Can angels be subject to death or mortal harm without the consent of God?

Indeed, there exist conflicts where celestial beings, such as the Gods presiding over warring factions, engage in a cosmic struggle. In such circumstances, the incarnated angels present in the earthly realm and embroiled in the conflict can indeed meet their demise without the divine will of their respective Gods. Yet, the primordial God refrains from direct intervention, as they have granted free will to all celestial entities, permitting events to unfold without direct interference.

424. Can incarnated angels be taken as prisoners in the context of a conflict or war?

Certainly, in the tumultuous backdrop of war, the conventional rules and restrictions lose their sway, and any individual, regardless of their celestial nature, can find themselves taken captive.

425. Can incarnated angels error or make mistakes?

Endowed with free will, incarnated angels possess the capacity to make their own choices, independent of divine counsel. However, owing to their limited perspective and incomplete understanding of the material world and its governing principles, they remain susceptible to committing erroneous actions and decisions.

426. Do incarnated angels always adhere to the truth, or are they capable of deceit?

Endowed with free will, incarnated angels may deviate

from the path of truth. They hold the capacity for deception, betrayal, untruthfulness, and even malevolent actions. Their concept of truth may diverge from that of mortals, and they may exercise the choice to disseminate falsehoods.

427. Can human beings ascend to a position of superiority over angels?

Angels, by their very nature, occupy hierarchical positions that stand above those of human beings. Nevertheless, there exists the potential for a mortal to ascend to a station of preeminence over angels, contingent on the manner in which they lead their lives, fulfil their personal missions, and advance their spiritual evolution. To draw a parallel, as exemplified in Christian prayers, it is said of the Virgin Mary that she is "more honourable than the Cherubim and beyond compare more glorious than the Seraphim."

428. Can angels become directly embroiled in earthly battles?

God, on select occasions, deploys angels of battle to intervene directly in earthly conflicts, with the aim of fulfilling divine plans. For instance, when God instructed Moses to ascend to the land promised to Abraham, Isaac, and Jacob, for God would send an angel to expel those who had laid claim to it. Similarly, when soldiers arrived to arrest Jesus, and one among his followers drew his sword in defence, Jesus counselled, "Put your sword back into its place; for all who take the sword will perish by the sword. Or do you think that I cannot appeal to my Father, and he will at once send me more than twelve legions of angels? But how then should the Scriptures be fulfilled, that it must be so?"

429. Can angels administer punishment to humans?

Indeed, they can, but only with Divine sanction. Both the Law and the Apocalypse were conveyed through angels, indicating that angels have the capacity to execute any acts related to God's grand design. In the context of the Apocalypse, seven angels are cited, each bearing one of the seven plagues designed for non-believers. Similarly, as Moses bore witness to an angel atop Mount Sinai, within the fiery confines of a burning bush. Angels wrought destruction upon Sodom, causing hail and fire to descend from the heavens. In another instance, an angel unleashed a plague upon Israel, claiming the lives of 70,000 people due to the transgressions of David, among other occurrences.

430. Who presently embodies the angel Lucifer?

The term Lucifer, when translated from Latin, conveys the meaning of "morning star" or "bringer of light." Lucifer was the second angel created by God, and He held a special place in His favour. Nevertheless, envy, ambition, and vanity consumed Lucifer, causing him to rebel against his Creator and harbour desires to supplant God. Subsequently, he raised an army of angels to wage war against the Almighty. After suffering defeat in the celestial battle, Lucifer, along with his host of angels, was banished from the realm of Heaven. This moment marked the initial fall of the angels. Consequently, Lucifer, along with his entire angelic army, forfeited their angelic forms, adopting various forms of evil within the material world, such as serpents, scorpions, and dragons. It is essential to comprehend that Lucifer no longer personifies Satan or the Devil, as he is conventionally perceived today. He is not damned; rather, he embodies a spirit striving to reunite with God.

431. Do angels of prosperity exist?

We have previously delved into the subject of angels of prosperity in the context of receiving gifts and blessings. Angels of prosperity are the bearers of wealth, well-being, and blessings, all of which emanate from the domain of the archangel Gabriel. These blessings encompass financial prosperity, material wealth, and even spiritual assets, including gold, knowledge, and health. In essence, everything quantifiable in terms of prosperity flows through the angel Gabriel and his legion. When we speak of prosperity, we encompass both material abundance and spiritual richness. Therefore, you can invoke the divine power of Gabriel through prayer and the kindling of candles directed towards him.

432. How do angels experience their time on Earth in relation to the people they encounter?

Incarnated angels are destined to confront mirrors of the individuals they once nurtured in previous lives as guardian angels. Most angels have previously descended to Earth, assuming roles as protectors and guides to human beings. Ultimately, angels are afforded the opportunity to witness the consequences of their prior actions, both benevolent and less virtuous, prompting them to embark on new incarnations. In reality, angels are drawn to the earthly school, cherishing the planet and its unique diversity within the cosmos. During their incarnations, they frequently encounter individuals who closely resemble those they previously cared for as guardian angels. Hence, the people they meet now mirror those they once nurtured and guided in the past. Parents whom they now reproach are, in fact, the individuals they trained and guided on the art of parenthood in prior lifetimes. These angels possess spouses who treat them as they were instructed to behave as either men or women in past lives. Furthermore, they encounter superiors who interact with them in a manner reflective of the way they were taught to treat subordinates in different lifetimes.

433. Can one possess multiple guardian angels at birth?

One may indeed be graced with several guardian angels at the outset of life, a privilege often bestowed upon those entrusted with a profoundly unique and extraordinary purpose in their earthly journey.

434. Did eminent historical figures who left an indelible mark on history require a greater number of guardian angels to fulfil their missions?

Prominent names etched in the annals of history were indeed notable incarnated angels or individuals possessing astral ages of great magnitude. These individuals were fortunate to have an abundance of guardian angels. For example, Napoleon, who remains unparalleled in history, acknowledged his significance, recognising that he mattered because he was needed by Someone. He once uttered the phrase: "As long as I was needed, I was great!" In reality, he comprehended that he was diminutive, but as long as he was required to be Napoleon, the man who established a lasting legislative framework still in place today and lifted France from destitution, he was, indeed, great. What set him apart and rendered him great were the numerous guardian angels assigned to him for his unique mission. Consequently, he was capable of juggling multiple tasks, simultaneously strategising for warfare, legislating, and even conversing with Josephine.

435. From where does an angel's soul derive upon incarnation?

Upon incarnation, an angel's soul is bestowed by the God of the celestial realm from which they originate as a spirit.

436. If an incarnated angel hails from a higher God than the one under whom they were initially baptised, to whom does their allegiance belong?

Incarnated angels owe their allegiance to both Gods, yet, through acquired knowledge and augmented spiritual power, they ultimately ascend beyond the God under whom they were initially baptised. Their paramount loyalty is directed toward the God from whom they originated and, most notably, to the Primordial God.

437. How many active structures does an incarnated angel possess?

The physical body of an incarnated angel embodies the cumulative structures up to the level from which their spirit emanates.

438. Do incarnated angels possess free will?

Incarnated angels execute God's will by choice and out of their desire to do so. Nonetheless, they retain free will, and among the incarnated angels, some, for various reasons, may become disillusioned with God and, exercising their free will, may decide not to heed the Divine will any longer, resulting in their committing errors.

439. Can the free will of incarnated angels be impaired?

At the juncture of incarnation, it is feasible for the spirits of incarnated angels to experience restricted or compromised free will as a consequence of their affiliation with the ancestral karma into which they have entered. Some spirits of incarnated angels may find themselves in a more diminished state, unable to exert control over the demons stemming from the opposite-sex parent's ancestral karma. In such cases, they exhibit traits that appear to fall within the autism spectrum, but are, in actuality, a manifestation of pseudo-autism.

440. How may incarnated angels reclaim their free will when ensnared by ancestral karma?

Certainly, if their free will has been impaired, they may exhibit malevolent tendencies, but their core nature remains inherently benevolent. Their guardian angels lead them towards various therapists, psychotherapists, and even priests who assist in their liberation. Upon severing ties with the demons that have held them captive, both mentally and emotionally, they regain their free will and commence the journey to express their authentic selves, aligning with the will of the Almighty.

441. Does the spiritual awakening of an incarnated angel hinge on their free will?

The spiritual awakening is not contingent on free will. The moment of spiritual awakening is a divine decree, and it can materialise at any juncture and location. The factors influencing the timing of this spiritual awakening are multifaceted and solely within the purview of God's judgment.

442. Who determines the spiritual awakening of an incarnated angel?

The determining force rests with the God from the celestial realm whence the angel originates as a spirit. Not even the Primordial God, the Creator of all, dictates the precise instant of spiritual awakening for incarnated angels from lesser realms, as doing so would infringe upon the free will of that angel's God.

443. Are there entities capable of overriding the free will of angels?

Indeed, any spiritual entity surpassing the angel's stature, including Gods, demons, and other angels of greater magnitudes, and even humans who have attained a higher level of evolution than said angels.

444. When does an incarnated angel attain complete free will?

As long as we remain bound by the law of karma, complete manifestation of free will eludes us. Under the dominion of karmic principles, encompassing cause and effect, we continue to exist within karmic relationships, karmic occupations, and even places of leisure, all intertwined with karmic obligations. As such, complete exercise of free will remains a distant prospect. Nevertheless, once an incarnated angel discharges all their karmic dues, especially those associated with ancestral karma, they emancipate themselves from the confines of karmic laws, thereby gaining the capacity to exercise their free will in its entirety.

445. If an incarnated angel fulfils their karmic obligations and transcends the law of karma, does full free will become their prerogative from that moment onward?

Undoubtedly, once they have settled all karmic dues, notably those stemming from ancestral karma, incarnated angels emerge from the jurisdiction of karmic laws and, in principle, possess the liberty to fully employ their free will. However, until they acquire an acute understanding of the distinctions between good and evil, they may make unwise choices, inadvertently reentering the cycle of karmic laws. The encouraging aspect for incarnated angels is their innate possession of a moral compass, which typically steers them toward virtuous choices.

446. Can an incarnated angel opt to forego the exercise of their free will and solely act in accordance with Divine will, even against their own desires?

At a certain point in spiritual evolution, incarnated angels may choose wholehearted submission to Divine will. Nevertheless, such a choice does not entail the forfeiture of free will; instead, it represents their conscious commitment to manifest the will of God to the fullest extent. A parallel can be drawn with the instance when Jesus chose to endure crucifixion. He carried out the Divine will while still wielding his free will, although he was cognisant of the impending suffering and crucifixion, despite personal reluctance. He beseeched God in the Garden of Gethsemane repeatedly, saying, "Father, if it be possible, let this cup pass from me: nevertheless, not as I will, but as thou wilt." Ultimately, he opted to embrace the Divine plan.

447. Under what circumstances can an incarnated angel forfeit their free will?

An incarnated angel may risk the forfeiture of their free will if they act against the Holy Spirit. In such cases, God may opt to strip them of their free will entirely, for example, in the event of a suicide attempt.

448. Is the free will of an incarnated angel impeded by negative programs, beliefs, fears, and the like?

Our shadow, representing the darker facets of our psyche, encompasses all negative thought patterns, adverse programs, fears, limiting beliefs, and other internal maladies. It constitutes a residual aspect that resides within our subconscious, harbouring negative energies that stem from our life experiences, ancestral lineage, and previous incarnations. This shadow element opposes our aspirations when we endeavour to exercise free will. Similarly, for incarnated angels, as with all humans, the healing of the shadow and the mending of emotional wounds are imperative for the release of constraints on free will.

449. Is the exercise of free will beneficial to incarnated angels?

The exercise of free will is not only beneficial but paramount. It is the essence of what God has created in us as divine beings. The freedom to act, create, decide, and make choices is the ultimate testimony to God's love for both angels and humanity. Love, fundamentally, is not coerced but consensually given; hence, free will is indispensable to the expression of love.

450. Did the concept of free will emerge with the creation of angels by God?

When only angels existed, their worship of God as the first beings, there was no room for the choice between good and evil, between light and darkness, for there was no duality. It was only after the fall of the initial angels, when Lucifer rebelled against the Creator, that duality surfaced, along with the capacity to select between two alternatives. In this manner, free will came into existence, affording even the angels the ability to make choices, with some opting not to serve God. Nonetheless, even these angels have the opportunity to choose to return to God at a later point.

451. Is an angel held responsible if they lack free will in their actions and deeds?

No, an incarnated angel is not culpable for their actions when their free will has been violated.

Entities of greater stature than angels, such as high-ranking demons, higher-level angels, and the Gods from their origin or above, can supersede the free will of incarnated angels, perhaps through magical means, for instance. In such instances, the angel is not spiritually liable for actions they were no longer able to control. This situation is specifically permitted by God for incarnated angels as a method for them to acquire humility.

452. What troubles can the free will of an incarnated angel bring about?

While God permits us to exercise free will, He refrains from prescribing what constitutes good and evil. As a result, poor choices can be made in our actions. The free will of an incarnated angel can lead to issues when erroneous decisions are made. If they fail to heed the messages their bodies convey to them—given that incarnated angels inherently embody the concept of good—their choices in a given situation can lead to catastrophic outcomes.

453. Is the free will of incarnated angels entirely voluntary, or is it influenced and inspired by guardian angels?

Guardian angels honour our free will but exhibit a proclivity to exert a positive influence on us for our betterment.

454. Are there incarnated angels who are never endowed with free will?

Yes, there exist incarnated angels who are devoid of free will. They function as custodians of karma, dispatched by God on a specific mission, akin to "collectors." They are akin to trams on predetermined tracks, diligently fulfilling a specific duty. This can be illustrated by figures like Attila, the leader of the Huns, who was famously referred to as the "scourge of God" because he was tasked with destabilising Christian Western Europe's foundations. Similar roles were assigned to individuals like Bayezid, Napoleon, and others.

455. Can it be asserted that an incarnated angel has acted with free will if they make an independent decision but subsequently fail to act in accordance with it?

Free will transcends mere contemplation of one's preferences. The essence of the concept was eloquently articulated by Dante Alighieri in his "Divine Comedy," stating, "The road to hell is paved with good intentions." Having virtuous intentions is insufficient. The ultimate criterion is the outcome of one's actions. For instance, if one endeavours to rescue an individual on the street through resuscitation, motivated by benevolent intentions, but misapplies the technique, inadvertently causing harm, their noble intentions cannot mitigate the adverse result. An incarnated angel's innate intuition, combined with their understanding of God's divine will, typically guides them toward choices that align with this understanding. Free will, in the context of incarnated angels, encompasses both thought and deed.

456. Do incarnated angels possess free will if they are deprived of liberty?

Freedom is not an essential precondition for the exercise of free will, except under extreme circumstances such as imprisonment, where one is unable to depart even if the desire exists, owing to the necessity of serving a sentence. However, in most instances, free will is distinct from freedom. Incarnated angels can exercise their free will even in the presence of limitations imposed by their occupations, communities, physical impairments, personal or hereditary karma, relationships, families, or other factors. They possess the autonomy to make choices, irrespective of the constraints surrounding them.

457. Is the free will of incarnated angels solely concerned with the choice between good and evil?

Free will is not inherently linked to the dichotomy of good and evil. It is centred on the prerogative to select from among two or more options, irrespective of their moral character. These options may even include two courses of action that are both virtuous. In essence, free will entails the freedom to choose according to one's preferences, uninfluenced by external factors such as moral considerations. Angels, too, exercise free will and can opt to follow or contravene God's will, which is why some angels choose to fall, opting not to adhere to God's divine plan.

458. How can an incarnated angel discern whether they have acted with free will in a given situation or not?

An incarnated angel may confront challenges in ascertaining whether their actions in a particular situation were genuinely products of free will. Their capacity to discern this hinges on whether their inner inclinations matched their chosen course of action. It is akin to a scenario where one's body inclines towards a leftward turn, yet they opt for a rightward one. It is in such moments of disjunction between intention and action that the realisation dawns that free will was not genuinely exercised. The complete expression of free will is contingent on the absence of any detrimental influences in one's personal sphere. This analogy aligns with the experience of peering through a window with smudged glass; the view is obscured.

459. Is the exercise of free will beneficial to God when it comes to incarnated angels?

Free will equips angels to make judicious decisions in the face of diverse circumstances. Each spirit, through the exercise of free will, possesses the potential to augment the divine realm. Ultimately, Earth and the entire material universe collectively serve as a comprehensive school for the edification and evolution of all spirits.

460. What transpires with incarnated angels who choose to end their own lives?

They tread a path akin to that of other souls who've succumbed to suicide. They are compelled to spend seven years within cells nestled in a prison located in the initial realm beyond life. Subsequently, they are destined to be reborn, embarking on life afresh upon the earthly plane.

461. Can incarnated angels, who have taken their own lives, attain salvation?

Indeed, they can, provided that other compassionate souls fervently pray for their deliverance. Through such collective supplication, they may be liberated from incarceration and, eventually, ascend from the abyss into which they've fallen.

462. What connection exists between angels and hallowed sanctuaries?

What does the term "holy place" genuinely signify? It serves as a gateway to celestial spheres vibrating at frequencies loftier than our earthly realm. Holy locales, these portals, serve as conduits through which angels descend from these higher dimensions to grace the earthly realm.

463. How do the angels correlate with the grace of saints?

The grace of saints finds its representation in the form of angels dispatched by the Divine to bestow recognition for the virtuous deeds of the saints and offer divine aid while they sojourn upon Earth. These benevolent angels may linger in relics or icons left behind by the saints, functioning as conduits for benevolence and guidance to humanity.

464. Which celestial beings make their presence known at holy sites like Fatima, Medjugorje, Lourdes, and the like?

Fatima, Medjugorje, and Lourdes exemplify manifestations of the divine feminine principle, heralding the descent of angels associated with the retinue of the Divine Mother. These celestial entities embody attributes such as artistry, creativity, and emotional healing. These sacred locales are distinguished by qualities intrinsically linked with the divine feminine principle: gentleness, love, tolerance, tenderness, sensitivity, harmony, equilibrium, and motherly love. Therefore, pilgrimages to these venerated sites offer a nurturing environment for the healing of emotional wounds and the rekindling of one's connection with the Divine Mother, as well as the healing and forgiveness of one's earthly maternal bonds.

465. What celestial entities make their presence felt at Santiago de Compostela?

Pilgrimages to Santiago de Compostela predominantly resonate with the angels representing the divine masculine principle. Consequently, embarking on a pilgrimage to Santiago de Compostela predominantly seeks to foster the healing of one's animus, the masculine aspect of the soul. This encompasses attributes like courage, persistence, unwavering resolve, and an unyielding determination. The angels accompanying the Divine Masculine Principle at Santiago de Compostela serve as instruments for the reconciliation of one's relationship with the Heavenly Father and for the forgiveness and healing of one's earthly paternal bonds.

466. Which celestial beings reveal themselves at the relics of saints?

The relics of saints are graced by angels embodying the sacred benedictions bestowed by the respective saint. These celestial beings, left behind by the saint as a source of solace and aid for humanity, serve as conduits connecting to the heavenly dimensions that the saint has attained.

467. What is the interplay between angels and pilgrimages to sanctified sites?

During a pilgrimage, one's soul is already attuned to the spiritual frequencies of that consecrated place. This means that every occurrence in one's life during the pilgrimage aligns with the spiritual entities, including the angels, presiding over the sacred site. Throughout the journey, the pilgrim remains under the protective and guiding aegis of these celestial beings, even when confronted with ostensibly adverse circumstances. The angels assist in settling karmic debts, facilitating purification, and overseeing every facet of the pilgrimage. These events transpire under the benevolent auspices of the angels, who manifest through the portal of the sacred site visited during the pilgrimage.

468. Could you elucidate the concepts of micro and macro angels?

Our universe is the universe perceived from the vantage point of individual consciousness. Micro-verses denote realms that exist within the confines of an entity or objects observable and comprehensible to that entity. For instance, a diamond, a crystal, or a stone constitutes an intrinsic micro-verse. A micro-verse can be likened to scrutinising oneself or an entity of comparable size through a microscope. Conversely, a macro-verse signifies a universe wherein a spiritual entity might perceive an entity like oneself only when employing a microscopic lens. In summation, angels inhabiting macro-verses are designated as macro-angels, while angels residing within micro-verses are referred to as micro-angels.

469. What is the relationship between angels and Christianity?

Christianity originated as a religion from Judaism with the involvement and intervention of Archangel Gabriel, who heralded the birth of Jesus. Hence, it is a faith inspired through angels.

470. When did the initial manifestation of angels within the Christian tradition occur?

The starting point for Christianity is often pinpointed to the Day of Pentecost, which commemorates the descent of the Holy Spirit, happening 50 days after the Resurrection of Jesus. On this significant day, divine grace, in the case of the apostles, signified the arrival of around one million angels each.

471. Is there a correlation between the hierarchy of the Christian Church and angels?

In the hierarchy of the Christic realm, God is symbolised by Jesus, occupying the pinnacle of both the earthly Church and the Christic realm, which is distinct from the primary realm of God and corresponds to our material universe. Consequently, all angels within Christianity bow to Jesus.

This obedience extends across all Christian denominations, including Baptists, Pentecostals, followers of the Church of Jesus, and others. In this order, angels are hierarchically under Jesus's dominion. The hierarchy continues with the twelve apostles, each of whom possesses their contingent of angels. Subsequently, they ordain bishops, who receive an assembly of approximately 150,000 angels. The priests are further down the hierarchy and have an entourage of 1,500 angels. These angels join the priests during sacraments, like baptism, religious ceremonies, anointing, communion, confession, matrimony, and prayers. Monks come next, bestowed with seven angels each. Lastly, laypeople, known as mirenii, possess the Christic baptismal angel. All angels are organised within this hierarchical pyramid, ultimately answering to Jesus.

472. How and when do angels manifest themselves in Christianity?

In Christianity, angelic manifestations transpire during the sacred rituals led by priests and Christian sacraments, encompassing ordination, communion (Eucharist), baptism, anointing, confession, matrimony, the anointing of the sick, and during Christian prayers. These rituals create conduits that facilitate the appearance of angels from the Christic realm.

473. Do priests receive angels during their ordination?

Within the ordination ceremony, which sanctifies a priest, the individual in question is endowed with 1,500 angels hailing from the level of Jesus. These angels pledge their allegiance to Jesus and thus designate the recipient as a servant of Jesus.

474. Is the number of angels allocated to a priest constant throughout their lifetime?

The number of angels bestowed upon a priest can fluctuate, contingent upon the efficacy of their priestly mission. Priests often referred to as being "graced" may witness an augmentation in the number of angels they possess, while others may experience a decrease.

475. Do individuals acquire angels during the sacrament of communion (Eucharist)?

The sacrament of communion, or Eucharist, comprises particles, information-energy, and spiritual essence derived from the entirety of Jesus's structure. These components emanate from the level of the Christic Sephirotic tree, thereby encompassing micro-angels from the Christic micro-verses.

476. How many angels are conferred during Christian baptism?

Christian baptism bestows upon the baptised child a baptismal angel sourced from the Christic realm, aligned with Jesus. In addition, the presiding priest, godparents, parents, and witnesses each receive an angel. The magnitude and significance of the child's angel may vary in accordance with the mission assigned by Jesus. It is imperative to acknowledge that the angel bestowed at baptism is distinct from the guardian angel received at birth, although it gradually becomes integrated within the individual.

477. Can a Christian baptised child receive an angel from a celestial level higher than the Christic realm?

If, during the baptismal ceremony, the baptised child, the priest, one of the godparents, the parents, or any of the attendees emanate from a celestial level greater than that of the Christic realm, such an occurrence is plausible. The heavens open to the highest vibrational level present during the baptismal ceremony.

478. Do individuals acquire angels within the confines of monastic life?

In the context of monastic life, and particularly during the anointing ceremony, each monk, upon receiving the anointing and pledging vows of chastity, poverty, and obedience, is conferred with seven angels from the level of the Christic realm.

479. Do individuals receive angels during confession?

During the act of confession, as the priest recites the absolution prayer, the heavens part, enabling the descent of angels during this sacred moment.

480. How do angels function within the sacrament of matrimony?

During the marriage ceremony, the heavens open, and with the "Dance of Isaiah," the Holy Spirit descends. This signifies that all in attendance receive angels, while the newly-formed family is bestowed a larger protective angel emanating from the Christic realm.

481. How do angels operate within the sacrament of anointing?

Within the anointing ceremony, healing angels manifest. During the service, the reading of the seven Gospels by the priests evokes the timeless healings performed by Jesus, involving the intervention of healing angels. These angelic forces become present during the service, resulting in the consecration of oil and flour, as well as the healing of those present.

482. Is there a connection between the number of priests conducting the anointing service and the number of angels present during the service?

The efficacy of a service is influenced by the number of priests and laypersons participating. A larger assembly magnifies the presence of all associated angels, amplifying the power of the angels, the collective prayers, the church's guardian angel, the healing energies, and the protective angels of those in attendance.

483. Does each church possess its angel, and if so, how is this angel received?

During the consecration service of a church, a celestial being is granted to the establishment. This angel corresponds to the spiritual level achieved by the individual who patronises the church (e.g., St. Mary, St. Michael, St. Nicholas, St. Paraskeva, etc.).

484. What is the role of a church's angel?

The angel of a church is tasked with aiding the church's priests, calling people to the church, offering assistance, protecting those in attendance, and safeguarding the physical structure of the church.

485. How does the power of a church's angel grow?

The strength of a church's angel increases with the performance of more services, an escalation in prayers, additional fasting, greater numbers of lit candles, and the conducting of more sacraments, including baptisms, ordinations, anointing services, and an expanded congregation. As time progresses, these elements collectively contribute to enhancing the angel's power.

486. Can a church's angel be bound?

Whether embodied or disembodied, an entity greater than the church's angel, or possessing more profound knowledge, a superior demon compared to the church's angel, is indeed capable of binding it. In the astral realm, a bound angel may appear as if mummified or constrained by chains, be it around the neck, head, hands, or feet—resembling the binding of a person on Earth. When bound, the angel loses its capacity to manifest divine will and free will, becoming unable to fulfil its intended role. The rationale behind binding an angel, aside from rendering it incapable of assisting the church, lies in the spirit's intention to manifest the angel's latent potential and power.

487. How can one discern that a church's angel is bound?

Key indications of a bound angel encompass a decrease in church attendance, a waning energy within the church, anomalous incidents occurring on the premises, the deterioration of objects, interpersonal disputes among congregants, and a perceptible lack of enthusiasm from the priest. When endeavouring to enter the church, a palpable reluctance may be sensed, or those particularly attuned might perceive the angel's sorrow, frustration, or even anguish.

488. How can one intervene or facilitate the liberation of a bound angel within a church?

Through prayer, purposeful candle lighting, Reiki, fasting, and a harmonious amalgamation of these endeavours, the angel of the church can be granted the strength necessary for its emancipation. For those pure of heart and knowledgeable, direct intervention is possible. Visualisation of the restraints (in the absence of a physical manifestation) and their severance with a sword of light is a viable approach. In the event of access to Archangel Michael and the requisite permission, one may invoke him and implore his assistance in breaking the bindings. Alternatively, one can transmit light, sufficient to empower the bound angel to surpass the entity that has bound it, ultimately achieving its release.

489. Is there a rationale for an angel associated with a church to be constrained by divine will or consent?

In cases where a priest or an adept employs an angel to assail another individual on grounds of religious, spiritual, political, or economic motives, the target of such angelic intervention retains the liberty to mount a defence and triumph over the dispatched angel. Through this act, the dominion over the angel, its potency, and potential becomes the province of the victorious party. While God permits the angel aligned with a person to engage in aggression, it is not indicative of God's volition or preference. Rather, it underscores the exercise of free will by both the individual and the angel in question.

490. Can we engage with angels through the use of crystals?

Crystals, due to their capacity to vibrate at frequencies higher than those of the Earth, establish corresponding links with angels, thus serving as potential intermediaries. Engaging with these crystals in conjunction with meditation constitutes an additional avenue to draw near to our personal angels or indeed any spiritual entities. These crystals function as metaphysical gateways connecting the earthly and ethereal dimensions. Their effectiveness hinges on their degree of purity and the frequency of their vibrations; purer and higher vibrational crystals facilitate more potent connections with stronger angels. The historical employment of gemstones in royal regalia by emperors and monarchs, it appears, was rooted in the desire to foster connections with celestial entities for guidance and support.

491. Which crystals, one might ask, may we employ to initiate connections with angels?

While virtually all crystals hold the potential for connecting with angels, those of greater purity prove to be instrumental in rendering the connection more accessible and, correspondingly, enhancing the power of intention and thought. Among the stones that have demonstrated a proclivity for facilitating such connections are diamonds, meteorites, seraphinite, angelite, celestite, aquamarine, prehnite, amethyst, selenite, and several others. For individuals less versed in the unique characteristics of specific crystals, it is possible to initiate contact with angels using crystals of a particular hue, aligned with the intended purpose. To illustrate, crystals of a rosy hue may facilitate communion with angels of love, verdant crystals align with angels of abundance, while dark crystals offer protection from malevolent forces.

492. What emerges as the simplest approach to cultivating connections with angels through crystals?

Wearing these crystals, having programmed them with the intention to foster connection with our angels, results in these gemstones becoming potent talismans. They engender heightened sensitivity to the messages relayed by angels, provide a tangible sense of their protective embrace, and promote their guidance throughout daily existence. Communicating with angels can be achieved through mental discourse, wherein we beseech their assistance in navigating diverse life scenarios.

493. How might we harness angels through crystals in the context of healing therapies?

Instances of heightened stress, emotional turmoil, or fits of rage culminate in the effective obstruction of the flow of vital life force, potentially resulting in ailments. Healing therapies, in their essence, pivot on the redirection of this vital energy, operating as a critical instrument in restoring the harmonious flow of Qi (life force) throughout the body. With angels on hand, the process of healing acquires a more precise and facilitative guidance. Leveraging crystals to access and invoke angels, it becomes imperative to adequately prepare oneself on physical, mental, emotional, and spiritual levels prior to the undertaking of therapeutic procedures. It is important to recognise that crystals possess the ability to amplify both positive and negative energies.

494. How do we elevate our mental state for therapeutic purposes in conjunction with angels?

Efficaciously establishing contact with a patient's energy field necessitates heightened perceptual capabilities, effectively accomplished through the energisation of one's mental state. Connectivity with the Yellow Ray of Archangel Jophiel serves to expedite alignment with a patient's energy field. For the activation of one's mental state and the augmentation of Archangel Jophiel's influence, clear quartz crystals prove to be of great utility.

495. How can chakras be purified through interaction with angels and crystals?

In the pursuit of purifying the aura and chakras, the use of a crystal pendulum suspended from a silver chain, the purity of the metal holding significance within therapeutic contexts, emerges as a potent instrument. The invocation of Archangel Zadkiel and the transformative Violet Flame results in the conversion of energetic impediments and released or removed negative energies into a positive energetic source. When gauging the state of one's chakras, conditioning the pendulum for responses both affirmative and negative, and subsequently hovering it above each chakra to assess the requirement for purification becomes essential.

496. Is it advantageous to enlist the aid of angels in sealing energy fields following therapeutic interventions?

Upon the culmination of therapeutic procedures, the importance of disengaging from the patient's energetic field and realigning one's focus cannot be overstated. In this regard, invoking Archangel Raphael to reintegrate, seal, and protect chakras and the aura stands as a valuable step, benefiting both the therapist and the recipient of therapy.

497. To which class of angels can we establish a connection through the use of diamonds?

Diamonds exhibit a remarkable affinity with the highest echelons of celestial energies and beings. This association has merited them the moniker "Invincible." Diamonds, like any other gemstone, encompass a range of purity levels and vibrational frequencies. Historically, diamonds have been recognised for their power to transcend poison, bearing the potential to remedy states of madness. These gems were employed to establish connections with entities capable of effecting the healing of afflicted individuals, often in the context of possession. Profound mystics within Judaic tradition have viewed diamonds as manifestations of celestial spirits. Diamond is utilised both as a guarantor of truth and as an impartial judge, owing to the belief that diamonds can alter their hue and brilliance in the presence of a transgressor.

498. What is the association between angels and the meteorites that fall to Earth, particularly those of substantial worth?

First and foremost, meteorites are composed of particles, information-energy, and spirit. On the one hand, they harbour demonic entities due to their material nature, and on the other, they encapsulate angelic entities, as matter is condensed in a particular form. If a meteorite possesses significant value, it signifies that its angel possesses virtuous qualities, and the demons residing within have ascended to a heightened state of vibration.

499. Is there an association between Reiki symbols and angels?

Reiki symbols serve as metaphorical keys that unlock gateways and serve as conduits for connection with a diverse array of planes, vibratory frequencies, and energies. The radiance emanating from these dimensions, upon entering our realm, is accompanied by various luminous entities, guides, and angels. An illustrative example can be drawn from Karuna Reiki, wherein distinct symbols establish connections with the energies of Archangels Gabriel, Raphael, Michael, and even the Virgin Mary.

500. What are the symbols within Karuna Reiki that establish connections with angels?

In the realm of Karuna Reiki, the symbols from the first level include ZONAR, which serves as a conduit to Archangel Gabriel; HALU, providing a link to the healing energies of Archangel Raphael; and RAMA, connecting practitioners to Archangel Michael.

501. How can one utilise the ZONAR symbol from Karuna Reiki to connect with Archangel Gabriel and for what purposes?

Archangel Gabriel, often regarded as the angel of gifts encompassing various forms of blessings, from wealth and love to clairvoyance and clear vision, also specialises in resolving karmic issues. ZONAR can be invoked with the intention of seeking Archangel Gabriel's aid in resolving karmic matters. By focusing on a karmic relationship or issue, connecting with the energy surrounding it, activating ZONAR, and subsequently channeling this energy towards Archangel Gabriel, individuals can implore him to assume responsibility for the associated karmic matter and facilitate its healing.

502. How can one employ the HALU symbol from Karuna Reiki to connect with Archangel Raphael, and for what specific purposes?

HALU acts as a conduit to the healing energies of Archangel Raphael, a divine healer with a specialisation in therapeutic practices and the battle against malevolent forces, including dark magic. It is imperative to note that HALU should be reserved for those patients with a sufficiently radiant inner light, as it triggers a healing ray that can be focused intently for both physical and emotional healing.

503. How can one utilise the RAMA symbol from Karuna Reiki to connect with Archangel Michael, and for what intentions?

RAMA, in Karuna Reiki, establishes a connection with the energies of Archangel Michael, known as the angel of protection and often associated with the realm of spiritual warfare. It is possible to perceive the presence of Archangel Michael when working with the RAMA symbol, particularly when striving to manifest goals that aim to assist others.

504. Do Reiki therapies encompass the involvement of angels affiliated with the Christic realm?

Indeed, Reiki therapies possess the capacity to open the heavens, extending to the level of the Christic realm, thereby allowing angels originating from the Christic realm to participate in Reiki therapies.

505. How do we discern which angels arrive during Reiki initiations and whether they bring beneficial influence?

During Reiki initiations, the heavens part to unveil the source of light in Reiki. These initiations beckon angels, often referred to as guides in Reiki parlance. First-degree initiation focuses on the palms, expanding to include the feet in the second degree. At the third-degree level, practitioners establish a direct connection to the universal source of light, a singular entity synonymous with the light of the primordial God. Reiki beckons angels from elevated vibrational planes, primarily those with healing attributes, as Reiki revolves around self-healing before extending that healing to others.

506. From whence do the angels in Reiki draw their luminance?

The angels within the realm of Reiki derive their luminance from the source of light within the material universe, adjusting the brilliance as necessitated. Engaging in self-treatment with Reiki, offering prayers, fasting, expressing gratitude for the angels, Reiki symbols, or other individuals, and the drawing of Reiki symbols each describe instances in which this source of light is illustrated. Angels imbue themselves with luminance during these moments. Certain forms of meditation, such as the Gassho meditation, are designed to connect one's energy centres with the source of light.

507. How can angels contribute to Reiki projects?

Angels, given their sufficient power, offer guidance and pave an optimal path toward the realisation of project goals. Reiki projects draw angels from various spiritual strata. By embedding Reiki symbols within a project and consistently channeling light into it, individuals also channel light to the angels actively working to manifest the project.

508. In what ways have angels played a role in the propagation of Reiki?

The widespread adoption of Reiki primarily hinges on its efficacy as a therapeutic practice. Reiki expedites what would traditionally take days to achieve through orthodox religious ceremonies, such as exorcisms, confessions, or the breaking of curses, often condensing these processes into a matter of minutes to two hours. Reiki, alongside the newer systems of Reiki, such as non-traditional Reiki, Karuna, Shamballa, Grand Master, Ascension Reiki, and Tibetan Reiki, facilitates rapid healing, including the breaking of curses, such as those associated with black magic. Healing extends beyond the spiritual, emotional, and psychological realms, encompassing familial relationships, connections with parents, relations with others, connections with God, and relations with the world. Consequently, the angels drawn to Reiki significantly contribute to the proliferation of this practice.

509. How many angels are received through Reiki initiations?

Reiki initiations are structured across various levels. At the first level, initiates receive four angels or guides. At the second degree, an additional two angels join the practitioner. Level three initiations introduce two more angels. Finally, during the Reiki master initiation, four additional angels or guides are bestowed upon the individual.

510. How do angels collaborate with Reiki in the context of healing individuals?

Angelic involvement in Reiki is channeled for the purpose of healing, whether through self-treatment for one's own well-being or as practitioners administer hands-on therapy or distant healing to others. In these healing processes, the Reiki practitioner acts as the vessel through which angelic influence is manifested.

511. How do Reiki angels aid us in comprehending the spiritual realm?

Angels provide guidance and support in our quest to grasp the fundamental principles of Reiki. They orchestrate synchronicities, subtly directing us towards books, television programs, or educational courses that facilitate our comprehension of the spiritual realm. Angels nudge us in the right direction, ensuring we encounter resources that nurture our spiritual understanding.

512. How do angels transmit their radiant energy through Reiki?

Angels within the realm of Reiki are intricately linked to the source of divine radiance, a connection that extends to the 10th level of the celestial hierarchy, associated with the Holy Spirit of Heaven 10. When a Reiki practitioner places their hands upon the recipient's body, a spiritual conduit is established. This channel extends from the practitioner to the angels and, ultimately, to the Source of Light itself. This transmission of light and energy operates on the fundamental principle articulated by Hermes Trismegistus: "the void attracts the full, and the full attracts the void."

513. How do angels work through Reiki to impact each chakra, aligning, repairing, opening, and harmonising them?

In the context of chakra healing, angels address imbalances and blockages. When chakras are blocked, operating below optimal efficiency, or misaligned, the energy channels are constricted. The practitioner's hands serve as a conduit through which negative energies are released or transmuted, thereby initiating a process of cleansing and amplification. The chakras are realigned to their intended positions within the human energy system. Symbolic representations employed in this process, which facilitate the connection to angels and the Source of Light, are instrumental in purifying, aligning, and enhancing the chakras.

514. How do angels cleanse and mend auras?

Auras encompass the energy fields surrounding entities, whether they are plants, animals, or humans. The process of cleansing and realigning the chakras contributes to the purification of the aura. This procedure is effective for various entities, including plants, animals, and humans.

515. How does one invoke an angel for assistance through Reiki?

Summoning angelic assistance through Reiki can be accomplished through a simple prayer or through the activation of sacred symbols. The act of drawing and vocalising these symbols, combined with visualisation, sends a clear and reverent message to the Reiki angels, beseeching their presence and intervention.

516. Do individual Reiki symbols correspond to specific angels?

Indeed, each unique Reiki symbol is intrinsically linked to a particular vibrational dimension. This dimension is associated with a distinct order of angels, each possessing their unique vibrational resonance and specialised purpose. The activation of a symbol serves as a gateway, inviting angels from that specific dimension to engage with the task at hand.

517. Which Reiki symbols can be employed to establish connections with luminous beings, namely angels?

The selection of Reiki symbols for establishing connections with luminous beings, such as angels, includes the Cho Ku Rei symbol, which aligns with the first dimension of light. Sei He Ki corresponds to the second dimension, Hon Sha Ze Sho Nen is associated with the third dimension, and Dai Ko Myo—the master symbol—establishes a connection with the supreme dimension, linking directly to the unending source of radiant light and boundless energy. In essence, Cho Ku Rei initiates a connection with an angel of physical healing, while Sei He Ki establishes a link with an angel specialised in the healing of the soul. Hon Sha Ze Sho Nen acts as a conduit to entities capable of instantaneously transmitting light and information across time and space. Dai Ko Myo binds us directly to the ultimate source of light and energy.

518. Is it possible to transmit or receive angelic guidance through Reiki?

Indeed, within the realm of Reiki, it is entirely possible to solicit or offer angelic guidance. When we find ourselves in need of assistance or answers, whether for our own enlightenment or for the benefit of others, we can engage Reiki symbols in a specific sequence. Through this process, we convey our needs or desires, signalling to the angels our request for their guidance and support.

519. Are we permitted to extend angelic guidance to others without their explicit request?

It is crucial to recognise that extending angelic guidance or transmitting divine light to others through Reiki should be undertaken with the utmost respect for their free will. Consequently, it is ethically impermissible to engage in such actions without the explicit consent of those involved.

520. Are there circumstances in which we can send light and angelic guidance to others without their request and consent?

One can dispatch light and angelic guidance to children below the age of 18 with the permission and request of their parents. Moreover, it is permissible to transmit it to individuals who find themselves in a state of coma and cannot provide consent, under the condition that, if it is not received, it is directed towards where it is most needed in the vast expanse of the Universe. For instance, if an individual has gone missing and cannot be located (e.g., stranded in a remote mountain area with no cellular signal), it is admissible to send angelic guidance and light under the same stipulation.

521. How can emotional impediments be disentangled with the aid of angels through Reiki?

Emotional blockages may be resolved by means of therapy targeted at the fourth chakra, which is achieved by laying on of hands and activation of chakra symbols. This procedure brings forth emotional issues to the surface, facilitating their awareness and understanding.

522. How does a Reiki master employ angels in therapy?

A Reiki master utilises hands-on therapy that is intrinsically connected to angels. The master applies a conditioning algorithm, which is expressed as: "May my hands gravitate towards where they are most needed for the bestowal of light." Alternatively, various techniques such as stroking, severing connections, employment of the staff of fire, laser Reiki, and scanning are employed.

523. How can one contribute to the alleviation of another's suffering remotely, with the aid of angels through Reiki?

Physical suffering represents an imbalance or an excess of energy. Through Reiki techniques that involve angels, one may either replenish the energy deficit or help in the dissipation of the energy surplus.

524. How does one establish a connection with angels to partake in distant Reiki practice?

A connection with the intended recipient is forged through the deployment of the Hon Sha Ze Sho Nen symbol in conjunction with the presence of angels. The Hon Sha Ze Sho Nen symbol embodies the concept of distant healing, constituting the transmission of Reiki energy across the dimensions of time, space, and distance. Through this symbol, angels are made aware of the timeless bond that connects with the specific individual in question.

525. How does Reiki energy contribute to the balance of karmic debts and personal healing?

Reiki has the capacity to transmit light back into the annals of the past, thereby serving the purpose of personal karmic healing, as well as tending to ancestral karmic healing. This is achieved through the utilisation of distinct symbols for the notion of distance and timelessness, exemplified by Hon Sha Ze Sho Nen. The process is complemented by the intentional act of connecting with angels.

526. In what manner can the energy of angels be harnessed to mitigate daily stress?

Persistent daily stress, if left unchecked, can exert a profound effect on one's mental state, emotional equilibrium, and personal sphere of protection. The secretions of the adrenal glands may be perturbed. In this regard, self-administered Reiki treatments serve to cleanse and reinvigorate the pivotal centres within one's mind, heart, and solar plexus.

527. How can angels, as channeled through Reiki, be integrated into the fabric of one's daily existence?

Angels can be invoked in a multiplicity of day-to-day activities, ranging from ensuring a secure journey while commuting via one's personal automobile or other means of transportation, to safeguarding one's own well-being, as well as that of one's family, one's dwelling, one's office, the devices in use, or the search for an optimal parking spot, an ideal meal, a suitable occupation, an appropriate remedy, an apt literary work, a proficient therapist, a capable mentor, a sagacious instructor, a prospective life partner, and countless other endeavours. One can adopt an algorithmic approach in this context, such as, for instance, when engaged in grocery shopping: "May my hands select the healthiest vegetables, fruits, and beverages for my benefit," and so forth.

528. What relationship exists between angels and kinesiology, divination, dowsing, and similar practices?

These diverse practices represent various methodologies through which angels, originating from the ethereal plane, communicate their responses to the material world. This is executed through the medium of physical movements, pendulum swings, or the manipulation of objects.

529. What connection can be discerned between angels and radiesthetic optimisations?

In the realm of radiesthetic optimisations, individuals are provided with guides, who serve to facilitate their radiesthetic measurements. The number of angels dispatched to a given individual is contingent upon the degree of proficiency achieved in the realm of radiesthesia.

530. Is it possible for angels to influence radiesthetic measurements?

Angels are the conduits through which radiesthetic measurements are conducted, which is why it is advisable to establish a connection with the Primordial God when engaging in these measurements.

531. Can demons utilise angels?

There exist exceptions where angels are defeated, taken captive by demons, and subsequently enlisted in demonic designs. Typically, these angels are of a youthful astral age and are often termed in radiesthetics as F.B.N.Es, signifying False Beneficial Noetic Entities.

532. What is the nexus between emotional wounds and angels?

The genesis of initial emotional wounds lies not with humans but with angels, their emergence coinciding with the Luciferic Fall.

533. How did the wound of rejection originate among angels?

At the moment of the Luciferic Fall, when Lucifer was cast into obscurity, angels underwent the experience of rejection. Consequently, angels who descend under compulsion to incarnate bear the wound of rejection.

534. How did the wound of abandonment take shape among angels?

Subsequent to the fallen angels' entrapment in matter, where they encountered the flow of time, incarcerated within the material realm for a prolonged span, they felt abandoned by God, thereby enduring the wound of abandonment.

535. When did angels experience feelings of injustice?

The angels who fell alongside Lucifer, although they were of such minuscule stature that they failed to truly grasp the proceedings, harboured a sense of injustice before God. This sentiment arose because they were penalised alongside the others, unwitting collateral victims.

536. When did angels perceive betrayal?

Those angels who descended with Lucifer felt betrayed by the Divine Feminine principle. At the crucial moment of decision, she failed to extend her defence or intercede on their behalf. She represented the Mother figure for all.

537. When did angels undergo the pangs of humiliation?

At the juncture of their descent, when their beauty, divine endowments, and potential were wrested from them, transforming them into serpents, scorpions, and dragons, they underwent an odious metamorphosis, ultimately subjecting them to the throes of humiliation.

538. Is there a connection between an individual's spiritual potency and angels?

In customary cases, an individual is bestowed a guardian angel commensurate with the benevolence they have dispensed in preceding lifetimes. The greater the magnitude of their virtuous deeds, the more formidable the shield of protection. Nonetheless, exceptions do arise. There are instances wherein an individual, despite a relatively limited record of benevolence, is endowed with a potent guardian angel due to exceptional personal mandates.

539. Is there an alliance between genius and angels?

Genius, a divine bestowment, is conferred through the agency of angels. It signifies a unique endowment of wisdom from the Divine. The phenomenon stands entirely independent of considerations such as religious affiliation, gender, age, cranial dimensions, or cranial size.

540. What distinguishes angels hailing from higher vibrational heavens from those originating in larger dimensional heavens?

The distinction centres upon the stratified composition of heavens nested within other heavens, resembling a succession of Russian nesting dolls. On each plane, angels exist, varying from the minuscule to the colossal. When a human ascends, traversing into a more expansive heaven, there arises the prospect of their guardian angel remaining ensconced within the confines of a smaller heavenly sphere.

541. Is there a connection between the moon and angels?

The moon, a celestial entity fashioned by the divine hand, cloaked in darkness, finds itself under the vigilant guard of archangels. Its purpose is to serve as the conduit for the sun's energy during the nocturnal hours. The moon, in the stillness of the night, enables particles and energy information from the sun to cascade down upon the Earth. This gentle moonlight becomes a means by which the Creator orchestrates the affairs of the night.

542. Is there a relationship between angels and wine?

The grapevine stands as a unique plant, possessing the remarkable ability to draw sustenance from the Earth and, with the nurturing light of the sun, give rise to a soul. Through the alchemical process of vinification, this soul within the grapes is transmuted into wine. Thus, wine carries a part of the soul. As wine rests in cellars, it accumulates the particles of light that emanate from the sun. These particles, as they pass through the matter, are akin to miniature angels. The longer this elixir remains in the darkness, the more light the soul within it assimilates, and these diminutive angels are transformed into a greater angel encased within the bottle. When we partake of this wine, we, in essence, become imbued with the essence of this particular angel. Thus, we ponder whether it is worthwhile to expend a considerable sum for aged and high-quality wine. And for what reason, you might ask, do individuals collect wine corks, the very corks imbued with this divine essence?

543. What are the angels in the Kabbalistic "Tree of Life" diagram?

The "Tree of Life" symbolises, on an ethereal and spiritual plane, the hierarchy within the spiritual realm of our material universe. Each branch of the Tree of Life, known as a "Sephirot," signifies a distinct form of creative force, and these forces are overseen by archangels.

544. Who are the archangels of the Tree of Life?

The archangels appointed to supervise each "Sephirot" of the Tree of Life are as follows:

- Kether (Crown)—personified by Archangel Metatron, the celestial conduit that links terrestrial existence to the divine energies of the Creator, fostering spiritual enlightenment and unity.

- Chokmah (Wisdom)—represented by Archangel Raziel, the bestower of divine mysteries and wisdom to humankind, helping individuals attain greater enlightenment and realise their full potential.
- Binah (Understanding)—governed by Archangel Tzaphkiel, this angel guides human beings in making practical life decisions.
- Chesed (Mercy)—led by Archangel Zadkiel, the angel of mercy and peace for those who offer their supplications.
- Geburah (Strength)—presided over by Archangel Chamuel, the angel of peaceful relationships.
- Tiphareth (Beauty)—under the watchful eyes of Archangels Michael and Raphael (who work in concert: Michael represents the divine angelic entity from above, while Raphael is the primary angel of healing).
- Netzach (Eternity)—guarded by Archangel Haniel, the angel of joy and jubilance.
- Hod (Glory)—again overseen by Archangels Michael and Raphael (who cooperate in their fight against sin).
- Yesod (Foundation)—symbolised by Archangel Gabriel, the angel of revelation, appointed by the Creator to nurture the foundation of the Tree.
- Malkuth (Kingdom)—ruled by Archangel Sandalphon, the angel of music and prayer, entrusted with conveying messages between the Creator and humanity.

545. Is there a connection between astrological predictions and angels?

Astrologers, particularly those of antiquity, did not solely rely upon the celestial constellations and planetary movements for their astrological prognostications. Those endowed with spiritual insight would, when called upon, receive assistance from angels and spiritual guides.

546. How may the archangels of the zodiac signs aid us?

Each zodiac sign is attended by an associated archangel, serving as a guardian and supervisor of the guardian angels specific to each sign. These archangels specialize in the unique characteristics of their respective signs and can offer guidance and assistance in various matters.

547. Who is the guardian archangel of Aries?

Archangel Ariel, the angel of action, is the guardian archangel of Aries. When Aries requires assistance in manifesting their desires, particularly in the context of tempering their pace and balancing their ego, they may invoke Ariel. Ariel is the instigator of projects and relationships, and serves as the consummator of actions.

548. Who is the guardian archangel of Taurus?

Archangel Chamuel, the angel of lost things, watches over Taurus. While Taurus typically focuses on the larger, more substantial aspects of life, they may occasionally feel "lost in space" when it comes to the smaller details. In such moments, Archangel Chamuel comes to their aid in recovering life's minor components, be they objects or modest joys.

549. Who is the guardian archangel of Gemini?

Archangel Zadkiel, the angel of divine forgiveness, serves as the guardian archangel for Gemini. Gemini's dual nature may often prompt them to seek forgiveness for their seemingly opposing personalities. Regardless of one's zodiac sign, Archangel Zadkiel can be summoned when there is a need for forgiveness, either to give or receive. Zadkiel also assists in balancing intellect and emotion when Gemini leans more toward the former.

550. Who is the guardian archangel of Cancer?

Archangel Gabriel, often regarded as the "maternal" figure of the angels, acts as the guardian archangel for Cancer. Due to their nurturing tendencies, Cancerians are known for their skills as parents. Archangel Gabriel provides support to parents in various ways, including financial assistance.

551. Who serves as the guardian archangel of Leo?

It is Archangel Raziel who assumes the role of guardian for Leo, a zodiac sign that frequently basks in the glow of the limelight. Raziel bestows upon Leo all the essential energies required for their role as the consummate showman. Raziel, as an archangel, fulfils the role of restoring equilibrium to the life of any Leo.

552. Which archangel watches over Virgo?

The angelic guardian of Virgo is Archangel Metatron. Tasked with the transformation of negative energy, Metatron's presence is indispensable to Virgos, who often find themselves wrestling with anxiety due to their aversion to drama. Metatron, as the archangel, extends a helping hand in the release from this emotional burden.

553. Who fulfils the role of guardian archangel for Libra?

In the realm of Libra, Archangel Jophiel emerges as the custodian archangel, an angel known for the mastery of Feng Shui. Libra, with its profound aversion to disorder, be it in the physical realm or amidst emotional chaos, finds solace in the presence of Archangel Jophiel. This divine entity specialises in the pursuit of harmony within external and internal domains, an essential attribute for the prosperity of Libra. Jophiel, the archangel, aids in transcending the chaos, uncovering the underlying beauty.

554. To whom is the guardianship of Scorpio entrusted?

Archangel Jeremiel, the angel heralding clarity, stands as the guardian of Scorpio. Scorpio, characterised by its profound penchant for paranoia, frequently internalises negativity, assuming it as a personal affliction. Within the embrace of Archangel Jeremiel, Scorpios find the capacity to perceive both facets of a singular coin, thereby unlocking answers to their introspections.

555. Who serves as the guardian archangel for Sagittarius?

The honour of guardianship over Sagittarius is ascribed to Archangel Raguel, the angel dedicated to conflict resolution. Sagittarius, with an aversion to discord and drama, manifests a remarkable flexibility and an enduring love for peace and harmony. In moments demanding the cessation of conflict, the invocation of Archangel Raguel becomes the refuge. Raguel, the archangel, comes to the fore during instances of hysteria or disputes.

556. Which archangel assumes the mantle of guardian for Capricorn?

Capricorn, inclined more toward the financial realm than spiritual or emotional matters, finds its guardian in

Archangel Azrael, the angel overseeing the afterlife. Azrael serves as a reminder to Capricorn, emphasising the broader perspective essential to maintaining balance.

557. Who stands as the guardian archangel of Aquarius?

Guardianship over Aquarius is assigned to Archangel Uriel, the angel embodying wisdom and sound decision-making. Aquarius, at times, becomes excessively ensnared in its thoughts and stands in need of Archangel Uriel's intervention to unlock their inner genius, for which they are renowned.

558. Who serves as the guardian archangel for Pisces?

The guardian archangel for Pisces is Archangel Sandalphon, who also governs the realm of music. Pisces, inherently creative and artistic, enjoys the privilege of seeking guidance from Sandalphon in the expression of their artistic inclinations.

559. Who guided Moses during the Exodus?

In the pages of two revered Jewish texts, the Zohar and the Talmud, a reference is made to Archangel Metatron as the celestial guide who led Moses and the Israelites during their Exodus through the wilderness en route to the Promised Land. This attribution stems from Metatron's association with the name of the Divine. The Zohar elucidates this connection, stating, "Who is Metatron? He is the highest-ranking archangel, transcending all other hosts in the celestial hierarchy."

560. What ties exist between angels and the legacy of King Solomon?

Following King Solomon's completion of a forty-day fast, he beseeched the Divine for wisdom. In response, angels hailing from the celestial sphere known as the Christic realm—specifically, cherubim and seraphim—were dispatched to provide their assistance. These divine entities collaborated to bestow the coveted wisdom upon the venerable King Solomon.

561. Can the offspring of the Divine serve as angels in the interims between incarnations or assume roles as angels, serpents, and the like?

After one's mortal demise, every spirit possesses the capacity to linger as a guide for fellow individuals.

562. How does one discern the voice of an angel from that of a demon?

Ordinarily, the voice of an angel assumes precedence when one is untainted. When impurity prevails, it may well be the voice of a demon. The voice of an angel may be discovered and cultivated through the practice of meditation, prayer, or in proximity to relics of sanctity, where demons are impeded from verbal discourse, among other methods.

563. What connotation underlies the declaration that "even angels have their demons"?

This assertion bears at least two interpretations: firstly, it implies that angels harbour their own imperfections or inner "demons," and secondly, it conveys the notion that one of the personal obligations of angels is to reintegrate a multitude of "demons" into the Divine fold by means of affection, assistance, and instruction.

564. Is it within the capacity of angels to entice and divert individuals from their designated missions or purposes?

Indeed, angels possess the potential to mislead

individuals if they so choose. There exists a proverb that admonishes against the "temptation of angels." This is because individuals may perceive the luminous nature of the angel, yet remain oblivious to the divergence between the angel's or God's true intentions and their own path.

565. Are human beings morally bound to heed the counsel of an angel?

There is no moral imperative that compels obedience to an angel; the human spirit retains its inherent free will. Angels communicate according to their level of consciousness or emanating from the Divine entity they represent, and as such, they may err.

566. Is it plausible that angels can be dispatched to assail our material Universe?

Indeed, angels may be dispatched by other Divine entities to assail our material Universe, often with the aim of acquiring spiritual riches or claiming souls.

567. Can angels from alternate Universes launch attacks on our Heavenly realms?

Yes, it is possible for angels from diverse Universes to launch assaults on our Heavenly spheres, particularly in the context of conflicts among different Divine entities. These conflicts may even culminate in wars of expansion among various Deities.

568. Can angels inflict harm upon mortal beings?

With the Divine consent of the Primordial Creator, angels may indeed inflict harm. This can occur when angels are dispatched by alternative Deities, by humans, or when they believe that their actions are inherently benevolent.

569. What factors contribute to the intensity of an angel's assault?

The force of an angel's assault is contingent upon the authority bestowed upon them by the Primordial Deity, or the spiritual potency they have achieved throughout their evolutionary journey.

570. Are human beings entitled to engage in combat with angels?

When angels initiate attacks without sanction from the Primordial Creator, but rather at the behest of another Deity or human influence, individuals are granted the liberty to confront and triumph over them.

571. What happens to the angels you defeat?

The angels you overcome become your angels.

572. If an angel sent by a God strikes me, how can I determine whether I should accept the punishment delivered through them?

You can inquire of the angel: "Were you sent by the Primordial God? Did my God send you?" If the answer is affirmative, you may accept the punishment. If not, you have the option to engage in a struggle and refuse the punishment.

573. If you are struck by the angel of a God other than the Primordial God, can you confront the God who sent them?

Yes, outside of my own God (to whom I am subjected) and the Primordial God, no other God has the authority to attack me. Therefore, I do have the right to confront the God who dispatched the angel.

574. Can we beseech angels to bring tranquility to emotionally unstable individuals?

Yes, angels can cleanse a person's soul, aiding in the restoration of their emotional equilibrium. However, we cannot intervene through angels without the individuals' consent.

575. Could angels have assisted the planet Earth during the pandemic and war?

Pandemics and wars are permitted by God, even if they stem from demonic attacks. Humanity must undergo them as trials, tests, and steps in spiritual evolution. Angels have contributed to both by maintaining balance.

576. Can we aid the angels in a manner that positively impacts the situation of Romanian society and, ultimately, all of humanity?

Yes, you can enhance the power of your guardian angel, transmit light to the guardian angels of your family, kin, country, city leaders, and so forth, and then extend this to all of humanity. Alternatively, through a black fast that generates spiritual gold, you can, at the end of the fast, request a larger angel in place of spiritual gold.

577. Why do angels help us?

Primarily because it is their personal mission given by God. If humans evolve under their guidance in the material world, they receive rewards, ranks, wings. Thus, angels evolve in relation to the spiritual evolution of the humans they guide. They learn, experience, suffer, rejoice, lose, and grow with humans.

578. What was the purpose of this book about angels?

The purpose was to make the existence of angels known, to characterise them so that humans can better understand them and know who they are dealing with. We aim to understand their likes and dislikes, to comprehend their needs and desires, and to assist them in their mission of having us progress spiritually.

CONCLUSION:

I understand that I may not have addressed all the topics or questions about angels, but I intend to find and provide answers as new questions or discoveries arise.

www.ingramcontent.com/pod-product-compliance
Lightning Source LLC
LaVergne TN
LVHW091323150826
845673LV00006B/1743

9786069721193